ARMOURED HUSSARS VOLUME 2

Images of the 1st Polish Armoured Division, Normandy, August 1944

Janusz Jarzembowski & David T. Bradley

Helion & Company

Helion & Company Limited
26 Willow Road
Solihull
West Midlands
B91 1UE
England
Tel. 0121 705 3393
Fax 0121 711 4075
Email: info@helion.co.uk
Website: www.helion.co.uk
Twitter: @helionbooks
Visit our blog http://blog.helion.co.uk/

Published by Helion & Company 2015
Designed and typeset by Bookcraft Ltd, Stroud, Gloucestershire
Cover designed by Paul Hewitt, Battlefield Design (www.battlefield-design.co.uk)
Printed by Henry Ling Ltd, Dorchester, Dorset

Text © Janusz Jarzembowski & David T. Bradley 2015
Photographs © Janusz Jarzembowski Jarzembowski (Armoured Hussars Archive, AHA), Polish Institute and Sikorski Museum (PISM) 2015 unless otherwise noted
Maps drawn by George Anderson © Helion & Company Ltd 2015
Colour profiles drawn by by Paul Hewitt, Battlefield Design (www.battlefield-design.co.uk)
© Helion & Company Ltd 2015
Colour artwork by Peter Dennis © Helion & Company Ltd 2015

Cover: 'The *Maczuga* (Mace) Hill 262N, Mont Ormel, 20 August 1944' by Peter Dennis. The reconstructed scene depicts an eyewitness account by the commander of the 2nd Armoured Regiment, of a close-quarter action, typifying the engagements experienced by the besieged Polish units on the Mace (the attack was successfully repulsed without further loss) – "At the same time a second group of 2-3 company-strong Germans managed to encroach upon our woodlet, surprising the tank platoon that had secured the L ridge, and attacked us from the rear. Preoccupied with firing immediately in front of our field of vision we became aware of our situation when the Germans started throwing grenades and several devil-may-care Germans started to actually mount our Shermans from 1st Squadron. This squadron started to independently withdraw their tanks. Some commanders started to fire backwards from their anti-aircraft machine guns, the tank gunners firing forward from their guns. When the anti-aircraft guns had run out of ammunition, the tank commanders actually pulled out their revolvers and tried to halt the tide of *Hitlerjugend* scrambling onto the tanks". Stanisław Koszutski *Wspomnienia z różnych pobojowisk*, London, 1972. Front cover, top right: 1st Polish Armoured Division insignia, worn on the left sleeve of the British issue uniform and painted on divisional vehicles (front and back). Designed by Captain Stanisław Glaser, 10th Dragoons Regiment, February 1942.

ISBN 978-1-910777-23-7

British Library Cataloguing-in-Publication Data.
A catalogue record for this book is available from the British Library.

For details of other military history titles published by Helion & Company Limited contact the above address, or visit our website: http://www.helion.co.uk.

We always welcome receiving book proposals from prospective authors.

Contents

Dedication & Acknowledgements

To my mother Halina and my father Aleksander, together again.

To my father Lieutenant Benjamin Bradley, Royal Artillery and Royal Electrical and Mechanical Engineers, who served his country, 1939-45.

The authors are most grateful for all the help and assistance they have received from so many people, in the United Kingdom, North America and Poland. However we would like to express our particular thanks to Ken Tout, formerly of the Northamptonshire Yeomanry, who not only graciously agreed to write a forward to this book, but also willingly contributed a section on Operations TOTALIZE and TRACTABLE in which he himself saw action and watched the 1st Polish Armoured Division enter combat for the first time. Ken Tout, military historian, was awarded, in honour of his work in popularizing the heroism of Polish soldiers in the Second World War, the Knight's Cross of the Order of Merit of the Republic of Poland, by the Polish Ambassador, his Excellency Mr. Witold Sobkow, on behalf of the President of Poland, at a ceremony at the Polish Embassy on 16 September 2015.

The authors would also like to thank Mr. Krzystof Barbarksi, Chairman of the Polish Institute and Sikorski Museum (PISM) and Dr. Andrzej Suchcitz, Keeper of the Archives, for access to their photographic archive. In order to assist it in the valuable work of honouring Poland's military heritage, the authors of this book are happy to donate any proceeds received from the sale of this book to the Institute.

We would further like to thank the following who offered invaluable advice and support, often at short-notice!

Brentwood Public Library: Anne Bruton, Mark Bullock, Bob Coelho, Val Cundy, Warwick Holby, Barry O'Brien, Sharon Ricketts, Julie Roffe, Verity Majumdar, Verity Newman, Nancy Redmond, Helen Riddington, Caroline Siveyer.

Tony Begg
Henry Budzynski (Stowarzyszenie Polskich Kombatantów Ltd)
Peter Cosgrove
Peter Dennis
Wojtek Deluga (Polish Institute and Sikorski Museum)
Marta Halama
Chris Jolin
Thomas Jones
Chris Lock (Lest We Forget Battlefield Tours, Flanders)
Henry Madej
Andrej Mazur (Pierwsza Polska Grupa Rekonstrukcji Historycznej w UK)
Paul Middleton (Miniature Armoured Fighting Vehicle Association)
Phil McCarty
David Paintin
Mark Pitt (1939-45 Living History Society 89 (Para) / 317 (Abn) Field Security Sections)
Marta Piskorowska (Stowarzyszenie Polskich Kombatantów Ltd)
Łukasz Stożek
Przemysław Świderek (Pierwsza Polska Grupa Rekonstrukcji Historycznej w UK)
Richard Szczawinski

Foreword

by Ken Tout

I was privileged to see the 1st Polish Armoured Division go into action for the first time on 8 August 1944. They passed though my tank regiment to expand the breakout from Caen. As they rumbled forward we waved our berets. Ahead, fanatical German SS *Hitlerjugend* men were fighting to prevent the entire German Army in Normandy from being cut off at Falaise. It was a desperate day.

Two weeks later the Poles would indeed link up with Canadians and Americans to cut off and destroy the enemy army. In that action the Poles won immortal fame at Mount Ormel. They went on to other significant achievements such as the liberation of Breda and the surrender of Wilhelmshaven. But before that they would endure a truly testing time in the two relatively unsung weeks from 8 August.

Overnight on 7 August my tank regiment and others had advanced across country through the German defences in Phase One of Operation TOTALIZE. We had seized the fortified village of Saint-Aignan-de-Cramesnil. At midday the *Hitlerjugend* launched a fierce counter-attack supported by Tiger tanks. This was beaten off almost as the first Polish tanks arrived to continue the advance into Phase Two.

It was not a propitious moment for tanks to advance across open ground against what were now the best trained and most motivated German troops left in Normandy. The defenders had the advantage of a very narrow, deep ravine through which tanks could squeeze and remain invisible to us. The Germans knew this ground well; so we and the Poles were at a great disadvantage. By evening more than 80 tanks had been destroyed, 20 of them German and rest from my regiment and the leading Polish units.

My regiment was ordered to stand fast in counterattack positions but the Poles were urged to push on. Again fate intervened in a peculiar fashion. The Canadian tank regiment due to advance two kilometres west of the Poles lost their way in the darkness, became isolated and by morning were surrounded and eliminated by the enemy. This caused Polish plans to be changed hurriedly in a hopeless effort to rescue the allied unit. Time was lost and men sacrificed.

It had been hoped that TOTALIZE would drive rapidly to Falaise. Delay was now inevitable. In addition planning had failed to note that streams which appeared on the map as narrow and fordable, were in fact like the previous fatal ravine, tank traps, which the enemy could defend with their powerful anti-tank guns and mortars. It was therefore necessary to halt, reform and plan a further costly set battle, named Operation TRACTABLE, against a determined enemy well dug in. Thus, even before that epic at Mount Ormel, the Polish tank men had travelled a true *via dolorosa* which had tested their bravery and skills to the extreme.

This album features many dramatic photographs from the renowned Polish Institute and Sikorski Museum (PISM) and is a tribute to those soldiers who fought so gallantly for Europe's freedom as part of the Allied Liberation Army. Many of the Poles already had considerable battle experience having fought campaigns in Poland in 1939 and Norway and France in 1940, proudly bearing the title of 'First to Fight'.

Brief warriors like myself, fighting only from June 1944, truly admire such outstanding soldiers.

Part I
First to Fight

On 6 May 1945, two days before the end of the war in Europe, a column of tanks approached the great German Port of Wilhelmshaven in North-West Germany. The tanks were American Shermans, their crews wore British Army uniforms, but the soldiers were Polish and their "winged hussar" insignia identified their unit as the 1st Polish Armoured Division. They were completing an odyssey that had taken many of them from Polish battlefields in 1939, then to France, and then in 1940 to the United Kingdom. There, as part of the Free Polish forces they had come together to form an Armoured Division which, after many months of training and preparation had crossed the English Channel to play a vital role in the closing stages of the Battle of Normandy. Then, over the following autumn, winter and spring months of 1944-45 had fought across France, Belgium and Holland and at last, finally into the *Reich* itself.

On the outskirts of Wilhelmshaven the officers in charge of the column met a German delegation of representatives of the German armed forces and civilian officials (wearing civilian clothes rather than their Nazi Party uniforms) for the official surrender ceremony of the port and city. After the conclusion of the formalities, the 1st Polish Armoured Division entered the town to begin its occupation duties. The entire operation was conducted in a totally efficient, disciplined and correct manner, a reflection of the high standards of professionalism instilled in the division by its General Officer Commanding, *General Brygady* Stanislaw Maczek who, after overcoming the defeats of 1939 and 1940, had founded, trained and then led by example the 1st Polish Armoured Division through its long period of preparation in the United Kingdom followed by its campaign across North-West Europe to its final triumph in Wilhelmshaven.

General Maczek was one of the leading (but largely unrecognised) Allied commanders of armour in the North-Western European Campaign of 1944-45. His expertise was built upon a background of wide experience gained serving in, or alongside four armies, fighting in several wars, and on many battlefields as varied as the Italian Alps, Polish plains, French hedgerows and Dutch polders.

Stanislaus Maczek was born in the city of Lvov, then part of the Austro-Hungarian Empire (now Lviv in modern Ukraine) in 1892. During the First World War he served as an officer in the Austro-Hungarian Army in a mountain infantry battalion. Here, where the swift interpretation of contour lines was of vital tactical importance he was able to develop his skills in military map-reading. He spent most of his service on the Italian Front where mountain infantry units played an important role as fast-moving shock troops.

At the end of the First World War, with the collapse of the Habsburg Empire, he returned to Poland and joined the newly revived state's army. The reconstituted Poland had to struggle to secure its frontiers, fighting a rising in Silesia and a war against the Ukraine. During this campaign Maczek was placed in command of a mobile "Flying" company based on the organization of a German *Sturmbataillone*, with which he would have been familiar from his service in Italy.

During the Polish-Soviet War 1919-20, Maczek was heavily involved in the fighting in the decisive battle of Warsaw in 1920 where the invading Soviet armies were repulsed, thus saving Eastern Europe from Bolshevism. In the following years Maczek would advance steadily in rank holding a succession of regimental and staff appointments. His last pre-war assignment was to take command of the Polish Army's first armoured formation, the 10th Armoured Cavalry Brigade (*10. Brygada Kawalerii Pancernej*), with the rank of Colonel.

Like many of the European armies between the wars the Poles had been grappling with the challenges posed by mechanization. Were tanks best employed in the infantry support role or as an independent strike force? Rapid technological development also presented armies with expensive and difficult choices regarding the level of investment that should be made in providing for these new armoured forces. Poland was in a particular disadvantageous position. It was a poor country with a limited industrial base, no natural frontiers and powerful enemies to both East and West.

Formed in 1937 the 10th Armoured Cavalry Brigade consisted of two regiments of motorized cavalry (the 10th Mounted Regiment and the 24th *Uhlans*) and reconnaissance troops mainly TK/TKS tankettes. The armoured element was provided by the 121st Light Tank Company equipped with British-built Vickers-Armstrong 6-ton (Mark E) light tanks given the Polish designation of *Vickers 6-tonowy*. The authorized strength of the company was some 10-11 tanks fitted with single turrets (mounting a 47mm Vickers quick-firing gun), together with five to six fitted with twin turrets (in 1939 each mounting a 7.92 *wz.30* machine-gun). Although the Poles did have a limited number of the excellent *7TP* medium tank (equal to the German PzKw III) none served with the brigade. The men of the Brigade wore a distinctive uniform with German 1916 model steel helmets and the officers wore black leather jackets, earning the formation the nickname of "The Black Brigade".

Shortly after its creation the Brigade had its first combat experience during a border dispute with Czechoslovakia. Following the Munich agreement of September 1938, Poland and Hungary both took the opportunity of making favourable adjustments to their borders with Czechoslovakia. Following an ultimatum Polish forces moved to occupy the disputed areas around the strategic rail centre of Bohumín in October 1938. Taking part in this operation was the newly formed 10th Armoured Cavalry Brigade under Colonel Maczek. As the brigade advanced on the Zdziar pass Colonel Maczek was informed by Colonel Duda, the local Czech Army commander that he had been ordered to defend the village of Zdziar. After consulting his superiors Colonel Maczek attacked. During the fighting Polish Army Major Stefan Rago was killed and a Corporal Oleksinski was wounded. Two Czech soldiers were killed and a number wounded.

Following this episode Colonel Maczek continued to test tactics and operational concepts with the Brigade but this process was interrupted by the German invasion of Poland on 1 September 1939.

The Germans attacked with a force of some 50 divisions, of which six were *panzer*, with a total of 2,626 tanks. The opposing Polish armoured forces consisted of some 95 modern *7TP* tanks, 35 Vickers light tanks, some recently delivered French R35s and 55 obsolete Renault FT-17 light tanks, some of which had seen service against the Bolsheviks in 1920. Several hundred TK/TKS tankettes were deployed amongst the infantry divisions and cavalry brigades. In support were some 10 armoured trains.

During the initial phase of the German Invasion in September 1939, the 10th Armoured Cavalry Brigade was attached first to the *Armia Kraków* and was in action almost immediately. Colonel Maczek therefore became the very first Allied commander to lead an armoured formation into battle against the new German *Panzer* Divisions and their new operational techniques.

Advancing from Slovakia, in the direction of Cracow was the German *14. Armee*. Its *18.Armeekorps*, consisting of the *2. Panzerdivision*, *4. Leichtedivision* and *3. Gebirgsdivision* would be the Brigade's main opponents during the campaign. A German *Panzerdivision* such as *2.Panzerdivision* had under command some 302 *Panzerkampfwagen* (PzKw) made up of 124 PzKw Is, 155 PzKw IIs, but only 6 PzKw IIIs and 17 PzKw IVs. Compared to such an opponent the combat power of the 10th Armoured Cavalry Brigade was severely limited with the small number of armoured vehicles at its disposal. Although the 121st Light Tank Company had an "authorized" strength of some 15-16 *Vickers 6-tonowy*, it would appear that its "actual" strength was only nine. In addition to its limited armoured component the Brigade also deployed the very effective *37mm wz.36 Bofors* anti-tank gun which came as an unpleasant surprise to the Germans. Most of their 674 tanks knocked out in September 1939 fell victim to the *wz.36*. The two motorised cavalry battalions of the Brigade were also equipped with the Polish *wz 35* anti-tank rifle, effective against the PzKw I and PzKw II which formed the majority of the German *Panzer* force at the time.

On 1 September in face of the advancing *2.Panzerdivision* the 10th Armoured Cavalry Brigade was ordered to hold the Germans in the Jordanow area. The village of Wysoka was defended by Colonel Dworzak's 24th *Uhlans* who held their positions against three unsuccessful German assaults. At the end of the day the Poles withdrew under cover from an armoured train. The Germans lost some 50 tanks. During these engagements Colonel Maczek handled his unit with skill. Both he and his troops were familiar with the area. At Kasina Wielke on 4 September 1939, fighting from ambush positions and making the occasional counter- attack, always taking full advantage of the hilly wooded terrain and its narrow roads, the Brigade, with the support of other Polish units, was able to slow, but not halt the German advance.

At Nowy Wiśnicz on 6 September the Poles were able again to inflict a severe reverse on the Germans. During the battle the 10th Armoured Cavalry Brigade fought against elements from *2. Panzerdivision*, *3. Gebirgsdivision* and *4. Leichtedivision*. During this battle a *Vickers 6-tonowy* from 121 Light Tank Company was immobilised with a damaged fuel tank. Lieutenant Michał Łukaszewicz the tank commander, and also 2nd Platoon commander, was killed, the other two crewmen escaped. This tank was the sole Polish loss of the day.

However, following the collapse of the front of *Armia Krakow* to its north the Brigade fell back towards Lvov, once again acting as a screening unit. The Polish High Command had hoped to establish a "bridgehead" along the Polish-Romanian border using that area's rough terrain of valleys, swamps and rivers to establish a redoubt from which a prolonged defence could be mounted, but these plans were rendered obsolete by the Soviet invasion from the East beginning on 17 September 1939.

Therefore the 10th Armoured Cavalry Brigade was ordered to cross the border into Hungary where it was interned. During the fighting 121st Light Tank Company had lost most of its *Vickers 6-tonowy*. Colonel Maczek paid tribute to their crews:

> ...In my thoughts I'm sending warm thanks to this brave company: for saving the day at Naprawa, for outstanding participation in the assault at Kasina, for doubling and tripling its presence on the Brigade's eastern flank, for they were supporting the unit's morale just with their presence; for they did not shirk from hardest tasks, telling, that they are only old, training junk.

Maczek and most of the survivors from the Brigade were able to make their way to France. It was hoped to be able to reconstitute a Polish Army in France and Maczek, promoted to Brigadier General by General Sikorski, Commander-in-Chief of Polish forces in France, was given the task of forming a Polish Light Armoured Division. Progress was slow and the supply of vehicles from French stocks limited.

When the Germans attacked France, Belgium and Holland on 10 May 1940, the division was not yet ready and saw no action during the initial phase of the campaign.

Following the evacuation of the British Expeditionary Force from Dunkirk, the Germans re-organised their forces and on 5 June launched Operation *ROT*, the campaign to finish off what remained of the French Army south of the River Somme.

In desperation the French demanded that the Polish troops be sent into action. Maczek realised that to deploy a full division was impossible and therefore organized his troops into the 10th Armoured Cavalry Brigade with a tank regiment with two armoured battalions, the 1st equipped with the Renault 35 and the 2nd with the Renault 40, plus an armoured cavalry regiment of two battalions and various supporting arms. The Brigade was first employed to cover the flank of the French 4th Army near Reims, where it helped in supporting the retreat of a French division. The Brigade first clashed with the Germans at Champaubert on 12 June. On 16 June the Brigade launched a night attack at Montbard on the *Canal de Bourgogne*, taking the Germans by surprise and capturing many prisoners. However, by now the French forces on their flanks were in a state of collapse, so the Poles were unable to exploit their victory. Surrounded by the enemy, short of fuel and ammunition, General Maczek ordered the destruction of the Brigade's remaining vehicles and equipment. Split into small groups, to evade the Germans, the survivors of the Brigade made their escape. To evacuate the remaining British and Allied forces from France the Royal Navy launched Operation ARIEL (sometimes AERIAL) using French ports along the Biscay Coast. Among the many vessels of all types used in this operation were the Polish liners *Sobieski* and *Batory* which evacuated Polish troops from the ports of Bayonne and Saint Jean-de-Luz. In all some 24,000 Polish soldiers were evacuated between 15-25 June. Other Polish soldiers, including General Maczek himself, were able to follow them by a variety of routes via France, Portugal and North Africa.

In Britain the task of rebuilding a Polish Army began anew. On 5 August 1940, General Sikorski, now Polish Prime Minister and Commander-in-Chief, signed an agreement with the British Government which enabled all Polish military forces to keep their national identity and military customs, such as marches and salutes, under Polish Command in conjunction with the British War Office. Of necessity the Polish Army in exile would have to wear British uniforms (with certain modifications to badges and insignia to reflect national traditions) adopt British Army staff methods, procedures and organisations. All vehicles and weapons would come from British stocks. In September 1940, the I Polish Corps, of six brigades and corps troops with an approximate strength of 15,300 was established in Scotland, where it assumed responsibility for the defence of the Fife and Angus coastlines. As there was concern about the threat of German invasion from Norway, Polish troops were active in building beach defences. As part of I Polish Corps the 1st Tank Regiment was formed and later expanded to form the 16th Tank Brigade in September 1941. The following November another armoured unit was created when 2nd Rifle Brigade was renamed 10th Armoured Cavalry Brigade with three infantry battalions.

In 1940 as there was a surplus of officers in proportion to troops, the Poles suggested the formation of a number of armoured trains that could be manned be some of these officers, provide useful training for future Polish armour personnel and play a role as part of the British Army's anti-invasion preparations. Eventually some 12 trains were organised and patrolled railway lines in Scotland and England. Compared with the armoured trains the Polish Army had in service in 1939, these were very basic. The locomotives were unarmoured, standard rail wagons were converted into combat wagons by the addition of metal plating and concrete. Armament included, Bren guns, anti-tank rifles and some were fitted with former World War I tank guns. As the expanding Polish armoured forces required more officers, and as the threat of invasion receded, the trains began to be disbanded in 1942.

The 16th Armoured Brigade was equipped with Valentine infantry support tanks. In November 1941 some 15 Churchill IIs were issued to its 65th Tank Battalion. They proved unpopular with their Polish crews owing to their mechanical unreliability and demanding maintenance requirements and were soon withdrawn.

Following discussions between General Sikorski and the War Office during 1941 it had finally been agreed to form a Polish Armoured Division. On 25 February the 1st Polish Armoured Division, *1.Dywizja Pancerna,* was established on the British organisation pattern. The British armoured division at this stage of the war was organised with two armoured brigades and a "Support Group" with artillery, anti-tank, anti-aircraft elements and infantry. This was the divisional structure used by 8th Army's armoured forces then in combat with the *Afrika Korps* in North Africa. In the 1st Polish Armoured Division the two armoured brigades were the 10th Armoured Cavalry Brigade and 16th Armoured Brigade. The Support Group consisted of the 10th Light Artillery Regiment, 10th Anti-tank Squadron, an anti-aircraft battery and the 1st Lorried Rifle Battalion. Regarding the provision of tanks for the division, Prime Minister Winston Churchill insisted to the War Office that "The Poles should be treated on this footing equally with British Divisions". The armoured brigades received the standard British cruiser tanks of the day, the Crusader, then in service with 8th Army in North Africa together with the Covenanter, an unsuccessful vehicle that was assessed as unsuitable for combat and was used solely for training in the United Kingdom.

To help him train and organise the 1st Polish Armoured Division Maczek greatly benefitted from the assistance of a cadre of experienced and talented staff officers, many of whom had served with him in the pre-war Polish Army and during the Polish and French campaigns. Colonel Franciszek Skibinski had served as Colonel Maczek's chief of staff in the 10th Armoured Cavalry Brigade from its formation and during the 1939 campaign. He was to serve as deputy commander of the 10th Armoured Cavalry Brigade, a brief tenure as temporary commander of the 10th Mounted Rifles before going on to command the 3rd Polish Infantry Brigade and later the 10th Armoured Cavalry Brigade. Major Aleksander Stefanowicz who commanded 1st Armoured Regiment in 1944 was a leading Polish expert on armoured warfare who had acted as a military observer during the Spanish Civil War. Major Stanislaw Koszutski, commander 2nd Armoured Regiment was a graduate of the Polish Higher Military Academy and the French *Ecole de Guerre*. Colonel Kazimierz Dworzak who commanded the 24th Uhlans in 1939 was Assistant Divisional Commander in 1944.

The 1st Polish Armoured Division was one of a number of non-English speaking Allied contingents that did not employ British Army staff procedures. Therefore, a British Army unit No. 4 Liaison Headquarters was assigned to the division to reduce any problems resulting from differences in doctrine, staff techniques and language. (In fact, because of the long association between the French and Polish armies, Polish officers, including General Maczek, were usually more familiar with French than English).

There was thorough and comprehensive individual training throughout the division. Some 1,470 officers and 11,114 men attended a wide variety of tactics and technical courses. Specialist training at the Polish Central Armour School in Scotland was received by 452 officers and 159 more attended British Army senior officer and staff training courses.

The Division was also able to participate in number of exercises during 1943 to test its combat capabilities. Exercise SNAFLE in the Newmarket area saw it "opposing" the 4th Canadian Armoured Division. Exercise LINK in September involved HQ 2nd Canadian Corps, 61st Division and 1st Polish Armoured Division. It performed well on these occasions, the division being particularly praised for its river crossing operations. However the assessment of the division after LINK warned:

> The Poles are so keen and work at such high pressure, that one cannot help feeling that while their efficiency may be unimpaired for the period of an exercise serious consequences might result from a prolonged series of action unless every opportunity is taken of rest.

Unfortunately most of the experience gained was lost, as shortly after the end of these exercises in September 1943, the 1st Polish Armoured Division had to undergo a drastic re-organisation.

Experience in the Western Desert had revealed serious shortcomings in the structure of the British Armoured Division. There were too many tanks and not enough anti-tank and infantry support. Therefore, in preparation for the forthcoming invasion of Europe, a new organisation was adopted. In future there would be only one armoured brigade. The weak "Support Group" would be replaced by a lorried infantry brigade of three infantry battalions. Artillery support would be provided by two field artillery regiments, one of which would be self-propelled. In addition there was to be an armoured reconnaissance regiment and the division would be able to call on increased levels of anti-tank, anti-aircraft and engineering support.

General Maczek was very unhappy with this change and the Poles only adopted this new organisation with great reluctance. It took time to implement as additional units had to be raised, and extra manpower allocated to comply with the new force structure. Also there had to be a reorganisation of existing units. It was decided to retain the name of the 10th Armoured Cavalry Brigade for the single armoured brigade.

Montgomery's British, Polish and Canadian armoured divisions would go to war with this new structure and although there would be some differences between them in equipment they would all be organised to the same establishment. In June 1944 a British armoured division had a total strength of 14,964 officers and men. Their armoured vehicles included 246 cruiser tanks, 44 light tanks, 261 armoured half-track carriers and 100 scout cars supported by 2,098 trucks and lorries. Artillery support was provided by 48 × 25 pounder field guns (half self-propelled), 78 × anti-tank guns (both 6 pounder and 17 pounder, some self-propelled), and 141 × anti-aircraft guns (20mm and 40mm).

The division's main combat elements were an armoured reconnaissance regiment, an armoured brigade and an infantry brigade supported by artillery regiments, engineers, medical and supply and transport units.

The armoured brigade comprised three armoured regiments. Each regiment had a headquarters including command tanks for the regimental commander and his immediate staff. He was supported by a headquarters squadron with an anti-aircraft platoon (troop in the British Army) with four anti-aircraft tanks, a reconnaissance platoon of 11 light tanks and eight scout cars for liaison. Each regiment was organised into three tank squadrons ("A", "B" and "C"). Each with a headquarters with three-four tanks and four platoons/troops each of four tanks. At full strength, some 18-19 tanks. However in combat these figures would vary widely as knocked out tanks were repaired and then returned to service. If the tank could not be quickly repaired or had been destroyed, replacement tanks, from the extensive Allied reserves, could be swiftly brought forward from the Tank Delivery Squadrons. Replacing killed or wounded tank crews would not be so easy a task.

The tank predominantly equipping the three armoured regiments in an armoured division's tank brigade was the American built M4 Sherman which had assumed the cruiser tank role. By 1944 this was the M4A4 version, known in British Army service as the Sherman V. The 30-ton Sherman was popular with its crews on account of its mechanical reliability (in contrast to many of the British built tanks that preceded it into service). Entering service with 8th Army at the Battle of El

Alamein the Sherman was state-of-the art in 1942 and fully equal to the latest PzKw IIIs and Panzer IVs of the *Afrika Korps*. However this was no longer the case in 1944. The British had already encountered the heavy German Tiger tank in Tunisia and later in Sicily and Italy and had actually been able to examine captured examples. The medium PzKw V Panther had made its (inauspicious) combat debut at Kursk in July 1943. There and in subsequent actions a number of intact examples had fallen into Soviet hands. However although they provided information, the Red Army did not supply their Allies with an actual example. In fact it was not until 24 May 1944, in combat following the fall of Monte Cassino during the advance on Rome, that the Panther was encountered in combat for the first time in the West. It was also not until early 1944 that Allied intelligence discovered, through PoW interrogation, that the Panther would be deployed to *Panzer* divisions, rather than organised in separate independent battalions like the Tiger, and was therefore likely to be regularly encountered on the battlefield. However the British had in development a programme to upgrade a number of vehicles with the very effective 17 pounder anti-tank gun which was capable of dealing with the heavier German tanks. These could be fitted on to a modified Sherman which was renamed "Firefly". To accommodate this much larger and more powerful weapon one crewman had to be removed (to make way for extra ammunition) and the rear of the turret extended, to allow for the extra recoil and for the installation of a radio. A major disadvantage was that the 17 pounder was much longer than the original 75mm and therefore made the Firefly a very distinctive target, despite efforts to disguise the extra length of the gun barrel, by the use of either paint or camouflage. Because of limited production capacity, the Firefly could only at first be issued on a scale of one per troop of four tanks. As it was felt that Fireflys would become priority enemy targets, tank troop commanders were forbidden to use them as their command tanks.

A reconnaissance platoon of light tanks was attached to each armoured regiment. In 1944 this was formed of 11 M3 Stuart light tanks. Supplied under lend-lease by the United States this 15-ton tank had a speed of 40 mph. It was fitted with a 37mm gun. First entering service with the British 8th Army in 1941 its reliability and effectiveness in the medium tank role earned it the nickname of "Honey". By 1944 it was totally obsolete. Many units actually removed the turret, substituting a 0.50 calibre machine gun mounting, believing that the 360 degree visibility this modification afforded was a more effective means of protection than the ineffective armament.

Although the Luftwaffe was a much diminished threat by 1944, it was still felt important to provide armoured regiments with their own close short-range anti-aircraft defence. Eight anti-aircraft tanks were therefore attached to each Armoured Regimental Headquarters. The Crusader Anti-Aircraft Mk II/III mounted a turret fitted with twin 20mm automatic cannon carried on obsolete cruiser tank hulls. As well as engaging enemy aircraft the guns could be depressed sufficiently to engage ground targets.

Each armoured brigade had under command a motor infantry battalion. This was designed to support the three armoured regiments. They were smaller (three companies) than the standard infantry battalion and usually one of these was assigned to each armoured regiment. It was more mobile than the normal infantry battalion, all its infantry being mounted in carriers and armoured half-tracks. Should the armour encounter opposition that it could not easily handle, such as dug-in infantry or anti-tank guns, it would be the role of the motor infantry to move forward to deal with the problem. It was also more heavily armed than the infantry in a standard battalion, with 12 as opposed to six × six pounder anti-tank guns and also deployed two medium machine gun platoons with a total of eight Vickers machine guns. The motor battalion infantrymen were issued with M5 armoured half-tracks which could provide some protection against small arms and shell fire and keep up with the tanks they were supporting. The M5 half-track was a variant of the M3 half-track already being made by White, Autocar, and Diamond T who could not keep pace with US Army demand. The International Harvester Company was therefore also requested to manufacture the half-track, but because of differing manufacturing equipment some changes had to be made to the design. This became the M5 half-track. Although essentially the M3 and M5 were the same, the M5 was heavier than the M3, there were slight differences in appearance between the two types and the armour plates in the M5 were welded rather than bolted. This armour was assessed by the Americans as slightly less effective against small calibre armour piercing rounds than that used in the M3. Thus the M5 was classified "limited standard" by the US Army and allocated to the Lend-Lease programme. Over half of M5 production (5,238) was sent to Britain where they served in the British, Polish and Canadian armoured divisions in a variety of roles; as transport for the motor infantry battalions, engineer and command vehicles, ambulances and tractors for 17 pounder anti-tank guns. The Red Army received some and the remainder were used for training by the US Army.

Directly under the direction of the divisional commander was the armoured reconnaissance regiment with a similar organisation to that of the armoured regiment. Equipping the armoured reconnaissance regiment in each British armoured division (and in all the armoured regiments of the 7th Armoured Division) and in the 1st Polish Armoured Division (but not in the Canadian Army) was the 30-ton Cromwell, the first truly reliable British built Cruiser tank. It was fast (35 mph) and manoeuvrable and felt to be particularly suitable for the reconnaissance role. The Cromwell was comparable in amour protection to the Sherman and mounted a similar Medium Velocity (MV) 75mm gun. Unlike the Sherman it could not be modified to take the 17 pounder. To meet this deficiency the Challenger, based on a larger version of the Cromwell hull, which could mount a 17 pounder, was developed but entered service only after the end of the Normandy campaign.

The armoured division's lorried infantry brigade consisted of three standard infantry battalions (with four companies larger than those in the motor rifle battalion). Unlike the infantry in the motor battalion with armoured carriers, the soldiers were transported in vehicles such as the Bedford QLT troop transport with limited protection and cross-country movement capability. Their role was to follow up the advance of the armoured brigade and then provide a defensive shield around the armour.

Artillery support for the armoured division was provided by its two field regiments. Each with 24 guns organised into eight gun batteries. One regiment manned the Sexton self-propelled version, while the other the towed artillery piece. It was recognised that heavy artillery support was essential to the success of any offensive. Although the 25 pounder was an excellent piece of equipment it did not have the range or destructive power of its US Army or German equivalents. However the Royal Artillery had developed very effective systems for artillery command and control and the fire support provided at the divisional level could be quickly reinforced by heavier artillery, such as 5.5 inch medium guns, or even heavier pieces, under corps or army command.

Each British, Polish and Canadian armoured division had an anti-tank regiment, each with four anti-tank batteries. Two batteries each equipped with 12 × 17 pounder towed anti-tank guns. The other with 12 US built and supplied M10 tank destroyers, organised into three troops of four guns. The US Army had, just before the outbreak of war developed the concept of the tank destroyer with the Tank Destroyer Force as a separate arm of service. The theory was that, while the tank would direct its effort at breaking through enemy lines, attacking infantry and artillery positions, it would be the role of the tank-destroyers, lightly armoured vehicles mounting powerful anti-tank guns, to hunt down enemy armour. The theory proved a complete disaster when put into practice by the US Army in Tunisia in 1942. By then the US Army had already developed the M10 tank destroyer based on a modified M4 hull mounting a 3-inch gun. Examples were supplied to the Royal Artillery who used them as self-propelled anti-tank guns. As with the Sherman, the British modified some of the vehicles to mount the 17 pounder and this modification was known as the "Achilles". Its particular weakness was its open topped turret, which, although this provided its crew with warning of approaching threats, made them vulnerable to small arms fire and shrapnel. However its mobility was a particular asset. To dig a towed 17 pounder into a prepared defensive position could take 12-15 hours. The M10/Achilles by contrast could be quickly moved forward and come rapidly into action. As the Armoured Reconnaissance Regiment had no 17 pounder equipped tanks, often troops of M10/Achilles were attached in support.

Defence against aircraft was provided by a light anti-aircraft regiment with three batteries each with six Bofors 40mm guns.

Each armoured division also contained an independent machine-gun company intended to provide extra firepower support for its infantry. This consisted of 12 (organised in three platoons) medium Vickers machine-guns. Although the design of these guns dated from the First World War they were very reliable and could deliver accurate and sustained fire in both attack and defence.

Engineer support was provided by two field squadrons, a field park company which acted as a base for the field squadrons and held specialist or bulky equipment such as bulldozers. The bridging troop carried the materials for 80 feet of Baily bridging, capable of taking loads of 40 tons.

To provide the communications necessary for command and control of the division was the role of the armoured divisional signals unit. It consisted of four signals companies in comparison with the three in a standard infantry division, the fourth being necessary to support the additional communications requirements of the armoured brigade.

Medical support for the Allied armies at this time was far superior to that provided for their soldiers by the Germans. The medical services of an armoured division consisted of one field ambulance, a light field ambulance, a field dressing station and a field hygiene section.

During the spring and early summer of 1944 the Division received a number of high level visitors, President Raczkiewicz of Poland, General Sosnkowski the new Polish Commander–in-Chief (following the death of General Sikorski at Gibraltar in July 1943), General Montgomery, to whose 21st Army Group the Poles would be assigned, and General Eisenhower, the Supreme Allied Commander.

Manpower was a constant concern of the division and was a factor in not assigning the division to the initial landings in Normandy, due to fears that it was understrength as well as concerns regarding casualty replacements once battle had been joined. The Poles planned to use German Prisoners of War (PoW) drawn from the ranks of those ethnic Poles conscripted into the *Wehrmacht* since 1939, as had been the practice of II Polish Corps fighting in Italy. However deployment of the 1st Polish Armoured Division was also delayed by the lack of room to deploy, so cramped was the Normandy bridgehead with supply depots, ammo dumps, and airfields, until the lodgement area had been sufficiently enlarged, and this had taken longer than anticipated.

Brought up to its full strength 1st Polish Armoured Division was mobilized on 19 March 1944. The division undertook a number of final exercises in the Scarborough area. On 4 June in the three-day Exercise NIEMAN the *24th Uhlans* conducted operations against the rest of the 10th Armoured Cavalry Brigade, and between 21-25 June the division exercised with the 2nd French Armoured Division.

Following these exercises the division concentrated in the Aldershot area during the second half of July and then moved to the ports of London, Dover and Southampton for passage to France. On arrival in Normandy the Poles moved to Bayeux where they came under the command of II Canadian Corps, 1st Canadian Army.

First to Fight

1938-44

1. Czech-Polish border, November 1938. Polish Officers from the 10th Armoured Cavalry Brigade are enthusiastically greeted by civilians. The officers are wearing their distinctive black leather coats that earned their unit the nickname of "the Black Brigade". Some of the officers are wearing the German 1916 pattern steel helmet, also unique to the Brigade. In the centre is Colonel Kazimierz Dworzak commanding officer 24th *Uhlans* (Lancers) Regiment, note his spurs. In Normandy 1944 Colonel Dworzak would serve as the Assistant Divisional Commander in the 1st Polish Armoured Division. (Łukasz Stożek)

2. Zdziar Pass, Czech-Polish border, November 1938. Troops from the 10th Armoured Cavalry Brigade drawn up along a road through the pass. In the aftermath of the Munich agreement of September 1938, Poland annexed certain areas along its border with Czechoslovakia, resulting in some armed clashes. At Zdziar, Colonel Maczek's newly formed 10th Armoured Cavalry Brigade fought briefly with Czech Army units, with casualties on both sides. The soldiers are wearing their distinctive German model 1916 steel helmet and greatcoats. The soldiers are standing with their motor bike and side-car combinations, light cars (probably *Lazik* all-terrain, door-less, four-passenger cars) and lorries (in the far distance). The crew of the motorcycle combination on the left hand side of the picture are wearing the French "Adrian" pattern helmet, as is an officer in the centre of the picture. These are probably from other Polish units involved in the operation. (Łukasz Stożek)

3. Poland, 1 September 1939. Invasion! A heavy German artillery barrage falls on the Polish village on the horizon, as the German Army launches Operation WEISS, its codename for the invasion of Poland. (AHA)

4. Poland, early September 1939. A German motorised column advances into Poland. The German vehicles are Krupp-Protze Kfz 69 trucks towing 3.7 cm Pak 36 anti-tank guns, the standard anti-tank gun of the German Army. The centre vehicle has a MG 34 mounted and manned for anti-aircraft defence and the vehicles and guns are camouflaged with foliage. A German BMW R-75 motor bike and side-car combination overtakes the lorries. In the distance German infantry advance across a field while smoke rises in the distance, perhaps from the objective they have just taken. (AHA)

5. Kasina Wielka, Poland, September 1939. Falling back after inflicting a severe reverse on on elements of the German *XVIII. Armeekorps* at the battle of Jordanow, (1-3 September 1939) the 10th Armoured Cavalry Brigade set up an ambush position at Kasina Wielka on 4 September where more losses were suffered by the advancing Germans. Here a column of pack animals from *3. Gebirgs-Division* moves past an abandoned Polish TK/TKS tankette lost during the battle. The gun has been removed from the wreck, possibly by its crew to prevent it falling into German hands. The soldiers are *Gebirgsjager* (mountain troops) wearing their distinctive *Bergmütze* forage caps and mountain boots. (Łukasz Stożek)

6. Trzciana, Poland, September 1939. A Polish Vickers-Armstrong 6-ton (Mark E) light tank (Polish designation *Vickers 6-tonowy*) from 121 Light Tank Company, 10th Armoured Cavalry Brigade, immobolised with a damaged fuel tank during the battle of Nowy Wiśnicz on 6 September 1939. Lieutenant Michał Łukaszewicz the tank commander (and also 2nd Platoon commander), was killed, the other two crewmen escaped. During the battle the 10th Armoured Cavalry Brigade fought against units of German units from *2. Panzerdivision*, *3. Gebirgsdivision* and *4. Leichtedivision*. This tank was the sole Polish loss of the day. (Łukasz Stożek)

7. Poland, September 1939. German soldiers pose with a captured Polish anti-tank gun. The gun is the Swedish Bofors 3.7 anti-tank gun, manufactured under license in Poland as the *37mm wz.36 Bofors*. In September 1939 some 1,200 were in service and its use came as a surprise to the Germans. Most of the 674 German tanks knocked out in September 1939 fell victim to the *wz.36*. One of the German soldiers wears the distinctive black uniform of the *Panzertruppen* (Armoured Troops). The other soldiers wear the standard German infantry uniform of the early-war period. The mixed nature of the group, and the goggles round the neck of one of them, probably indicate that they are all from a *Panzerdivision*. The tank crewman from a Panzer Regiment, the others from one of the division's motorized *Schutzen* (Rifle) Regiments, a designation intended to distinguish them from the infantrymen serving in the standard "foot" infantry divisions. They were redesignated as *Panzer Grenadiers* in 1942. (AHA)

8. Poland, September 1939. A knocked-out or abandoned Polish 7TP (*dwuwiezowy*-twin turret) light tank. Adapted from a British Vickers design and license-built in Poland, 40 were fitted with two turrets each mounting a machine gun. This one has had one of these guns removed. A further 95 were equipped with a single turret mounting a Bofors 37mm gun (see photo 9). (AHA)

9. Poland, September 1939. An abandoned Polish 7TP (*jednowieżowy*-single turret) light tank belonging to either the 2nd or 3rd light tank battalion. With a diesel engine and fitted with a Bofors 37mm gun it was superior to the majority of German tanks encountered, particularly the PzKw II, as was demonstrated on 4th September 1939 when Captain Antoni Prochniewicz of the 2nd Light Tank Battalion successfully engaged a number of PzKw II tanks from 1. *Panzerdivision* at Gaski. Later Captain Prochniewicz fell into Soviet captivity and was one of the 22,000 Polish officers murdered in the Katyn Forest. (AHA)

10. Zabinka Railway Station, Poland, 14 September 1939. German soldiers examine an abandoned Polish FT-17 light tank from Polish Armoured Train *Bartosz Glowack* (named after a peasant hero of the 1794 Kosciuszko Insurrection against the Russians). The tank usually operated on a *Draisine*, auxiliary rail vehicle. An armoured vehicle could sit on the *Draisine* and move it along the railway tracks using its own power. The tank could be dismounted from its *Draisine* allowing it to operate as normal. In 1939 each Polish Armoured train included two Renault FT-17 *Draisines* and four TSK *Draisines* as part of its complement. (AHA)

11. Zabinka, Poland, 14 September 1939. On 14 September *Bartosz Glowack* went into action against units from the *3.Panzerdivision* at the strategic railway station at Zabinka. The train dismounted its TKS tankettes, three of which were later knocked out (see photo 12). A Renault was also dismounted and this is the vehicle seen here and in photo 10. It may have been deliberately abandoned in an effort to block the track. Here a German NCO watches as some of his comrades, probably from the 3.*Panzerdivision,* attempt to move the Renault and thus free the use of the railway line for their own forces. The German soldier in the centre is wearing the long rubberized protective coat issued to motorcycle riders. (AHA)

12. Zabinka, Poland, 14 September 1939. A German soldier examines two knocked out TKS tankettes. These are two of the three TKS tankettes from *Bartosz Glowack* knocked out in fighting with German armoured cars near Zabinka Railway Station. The Polish Army deployed some 450 TK/TKS tankettes in 1939, most were armed with 7.92 machine guns, but some 40 were equipped with a potent 20mm anti-tank cannon. (AHA)

13. Poland, September 1939. Some of the 400,000 Polish PoWs captured by the German (over 200,000 by the Soviets), some wounded, march into captivity. There was no Polish national capitulation, but many Polish soldiers were forced to surrender during the campaign, only to face an uncertain future as forced labourers or enlistment into the German army, in order to survive. As the Poles march to the rear a German horse-drawn supply column moves forward. In 1939, despite the propaganda image, the majority of the German Army still marched on foot, with much of its artillery and supply wagons horse-drawn. (AHA)

14. Poland, September 1939. A horse-drawn cart filled with civilian men, women and children approach a road-block where a German armoured car has trained its turret mounted canon and machine gun on them. The eight-wheeled armoured car is a Sd.Kfz 232 armoured radio car (the metal structure mounted on top of the vehicle is a radio aerial), a variant of the standard Sd.Kfz 231. Both vehicles were widely used by German Panzer divisions for reconnaissance. On the side of the vehicle is a white Balkan cross, the standard German army insignia in 1939. It was replaced after the Polish campaign by the more familiar, and less conspicuous, black cross with white outline. (AHA)

15. Hungary, September 1939. Some 1500 survivors (from the original 3,000) of the 10th Armoured Cavalry Brigade, together with their remaining equipment crossed into Hungary through the Tatar Pass (now the Yablonitsky Pass in Ukraine) on 19 September and were interned. The vehicles, such as these tankettes, were taken over by the Hungarian Army. The Polish tankettes include two TKS with 20mm cannon (left) and to the right, two TKF (note the different shape of the front suspension connector distinguishing them from the TKS), the "F" in the vehicle designation indicated the fitting of a Fiat engine. In the background are a number of Polish trucks built by the Ursus plant in Warsaw. (PISM)

16. Camp de Bressuire, France, February 1940. Polish soldiers, part of the 35,000 which managed to reach France, some of whom are dressed in their newly-issued French uniforms, with Polish insignia on their forage caps, pose for a photo. A.L Jarzembowski, NCO, *1st Battalion Chars de Combat* (1st Tank Battalion) is in civilian clothes, third from left. (AHA)

17. France, June 1940. Renault R-35 infantry tanks from the 1st Tank battalion, 10th Armoured Cavalry Brigade move down a French road. The 2nd battalion was equipped with the Renault R-40. In June 1940 the Brigade was rushed into battle, not fully operational. Although enjoying some initial success the Poles were engulfed in the general collapse of the French armies. As a result of fuel and ammunition shortages most of the vehicles and equipment were destroyed and the troops ordered to make their way to Great Britain and some 19,000 were able to do this by a variety of routes.
(*2nd Polish Armoured Regiment in Action, From Caen to Wihelmshaven. Tadeusz Wiatrowski, Schlutersche Buchdrucferei, Hannover 1946*)

18. Operational ARIEL, Verdon-sur-Mer, France, June 1940. Polish troops arrive at the French Port of Verdon-sur-Mer, at the mouth of the Gironde Estuary, for evacuation to Great Britain. Before departure, they return their French-issue military equipment. A group of officers stand by the lorries belonging to 10th Mounted Rifles part of the 10th Armoured Cavalry Brigade. The soldiers wear a mixture of uniforms (some items of which they would continue to wear for some time in Great Britain). Some are infantry. Operation ARIEL (sometimes AERIAL) 20-25 June 1940, was the Royal Navy evacuation of some 191,870 British and allied military and civilian personnel from the French Biscay ports, immediately before the French surrender. Particular attention was given to the military forces that had been established in France by the Polish and Czech governments-in-exile. On 22 June the merchant ships *Clan Ferguson* and *Royal Scotsman* sailed from Verdon for Liverpool with 10,000 Polish troops aboard. On 23 June the merchantman *Delius* evacuated a further 6,000 before the port was abandoned. (PISM).

Birth of a Division

1940-44

19. Crawford Camp, South Lanarkshire, Scotland 1940. Polish soldiers, newly arrived from the continent and dressed in their French uniforms, admire a welcoming group of Scottish pipers from the Cameronians (Scottish Rifles). On the 25 June 1940 orders were issued for the formation of a Polish Armoured unit with Crawford becoming the Polish Armoured Forces Centre. This was followed with the creation of the Polish 1st Corps in October 1940 based at Perth. (AHA)

20. Stonyburn, West Lothian, Scotland 9 August 1940. Polish troops still in their French-issue uniforms reflect on home, with Sergeant Major A.L.Jarzembowski, extreme right. Note a member of the 10th Cavalry Brigade, dressed in his black leather coat in the left background. (AHA)

21. Valentine tanks, Scotland early 1942. A column of Mk III Valentine II infantry tanks halts on manoeuvres. The vehicles are from the 66th Tank Battalion, 16th Armoured Brigade, I Polish Corps. Note the Michelin Man figure mascot on turret. The Valentine was manufactured both in Great Britain and Canada and was the most produced British tank of the war and saw extensive service across many theatres; with the 1st and 8th Armies in North Africa, with the Red Army on the Eastern Front and with the New Zealand Army in the Pacific. (AHA)

22. Valentine tank, Scotland early 1942. Another Valentine from the column shown in photo 21. The Valentine Mk II mounted a 2 pounder gun and was manned by a crew of three. The crew are seen still wearing their French issued uniforms including the motorised troopers helmet and the brown leather jacket (both 1935 pattern) issued to armoured crews. The markings on the front hull are. Left to right, PL, Poland, 16, bridge classification tonnage number, 073, 66thTank Battalion, and the circle/wing, 1 Polish Corps. (AHA)

23. General Wladyslaw Sikorski (1881-1943), Blairgowrie, Scotland, 1942. Accompanied by with General Marian Kukiel (1885-1972) commanding Officer I Polish Corps, 1940-42 and then Polish Minister of War, 1942-49, talking to infantrymen, probably from the 16th Dragoon Battalion which was raised as the brigade's integral motor battalion following British army organisation and practice. All the soldiers are wearing standard British issue battledress and equipment and have the Polish national insignia, a yellow painted eagle, stenciled on their helmets. (AHA)

24. Valentine tank, Scotland early 1942. Polish tank crew men pose or rest alongside a Valentine infantry tank, from the 66 Battalion, 16th Armoured Brigade, I Polish Corps, during a halt on manoeuvres. The tank crews are wearing French Army issue uniforms. However the bare headed soldier in the centre is wearing a British Army motorcyclist's protective rubberized wet weather uniform as well as a long bayonet scabbard for the British Short Magazine Lee Enfield (SMLE) rifle. (AHA)

25. Armoured crews, Scotland early 1942. Valentine crews being briefed. French leather jackets are in evidence, however the soldier on the right is in British Army Battledress. The ranks are displayed on their berets, a Lance Corporal (one bar), a Corporal (two bars), a Lance Sergeant (three bars), a Sergeant (a chevron), a Second Lieutenant (one star) and a Lieutenant (two stars). Note also the Michelin Man mascot on the tank turret which can also be seen in photo 21. (AHA)

26. Tank transporter, Scotland, 1942. An Infantry Tank Mk II Valentine II of the 16th Armoured Brigade, I Polish Corps being carried on a White-Ruxtall 922 18 ton 6 × 4 drive tank transporter. These US vehicles were originally ordered for the French Army but later diverted to Britain where the tank transporter bodies were added. This vehicle is also part of the Corps as indicated by the PL (Poland) marking on the left mudguard. The number "40" on the disc in front is the bridge classification sign and would be in yellow. The soldier on the extreme left of the picture may be part of the tank crew as he is wearing a 1940 Non-Crash Helmet, Royal Tank Corps. The three soldiers on the right of the photo are wearing rain capes. (PISM)

27. Anti-invasion fortification, Scotland, 1940. Polish soldiers inspect a BL 6 inch Mk VII, a type that was used extensively for long-range bombardment during World War I. Although some 330,000 BEF and allied troops were evacuated from Dunkirk, all their heavy equipment, particularly artillery had to be abandoned. Until these losses could be replaced, obsolete guns (such as this example) were removed from storage to coastal defence emplacements. After their evacuation from France the Poles were posted to Scotland to construct and man local defences along the Fife and Angus coastlines in case of any German assault from the direction of Norway, and these Polish soldiers may well be learning how to operate this particular gun should invasion come. (Marta Piskorowska)

28. 10th Mounted Rifles, Cupar, Fife, Scotland 23 October 1940. Officers and men of the 1st Rifle Battalion parade with their standard. Although only in the United Kingdom for a few months the troops are wearing British uniforms and helmets and carrying British SMLE rifles. Following his arrival in the United Kingdom, General Maczek had been appointed commander of 2nd Rifle Brigade which in November 1940 was redesignated as the 10th Armoured Cavalry Brigade. In 1941 the brigade consisted of three rifle battalions. Traditional Polish Army unit names were assigned to these battalion on an unofficial basis with the 1st Rifle Battalion being renamed the 10th Mounted Rifles. It would eventually become the 1st Polish Armoured Division's Armoured Reconnaissance Regiment. (Marta Piskorowska)

29. Winston Churchill, Cupar, Fife, Scotland, 23 October 1940. The Prime Minister, accompanied by General Sikorski inspect Polish troops during a visit to Scotland. The Headquarters of the 1st Polish Rifle Brigade was at Cupar and its 2nd Rifle battalion was also stationed there. Both Prime Ministers are accompanied by other British and Polish officers. The Polish soldiers, probably from 2nd battalion are in British uniform but appear to have the rifles slung in the Polish version of "present arms" and are wearing capes. General Sikorski had a long and distinguished military career, serving first in the Austro-Hungarian Army during World War I and later in Pilsudki's Legion. He commanded an army in the Polish-Soviet War (1919-1921) but following Pilsudski's coup in May 1926 he held no further military appointments before the war. After the defeat of Poland in 1939 and the fall of France in 1940, Sikorski established the Polish Government in exile in London with the appointments of both Prime Minister and Commander in Chief. It was a tragedy for his country when Sikorski was killed on 4 July 1943, his aircraft crashing while taking off from the airfield at Gibraltar. (AHA)

30. Winston Churchill, Cupar, Fife, Scotland, 23 October 1940. The inspection appears to have ended and Mrs. Churchill has joined her husband and General Sikorski (to the left). A Polish officer has made Mrs. Churchill a loan of his coat, perhaps as added protection against the obviously inclement weather. Mr. and Mrs. Churchill, together with General Sikorski, listen intently to a briefing given by the Polish officer at the extreme right of the picture. They are accompanied by a mixture of British and Polish officers. Those wearing steel helmets will be Polish and associated with the troops being inspected. (AHA)

31. Royal Visit, Angus County Buildings, Market Street, Forfar, Scotland, 23 April 1941 (sequential photos 31-33). King George VI and Queen Elizabeth, together with General Sikorski, take the salute at a march-past of Polish Soldiers during a visit to Scotland. The saluting base is decorated with the Union and Polish flags and the Polish Eagle national emblem. With the Royal party and General Sikorski are other senior British and Polish officers and civilian officials. On the terrace above, staff cars await in readiness for the VIPs. Note the heavily sandbagged windows offering some protection against air raids, in the building behind. (AHA)

32. Royal Visit, Forfar, Scotland, 23 April 1941. Polish troops about to march past King George VI, Queen Elizabeth and General Sikorski. Although the soldiers are wearing British uniform they are marching and carrying their rifles in traditional Polish Army style. (AHA)

33. Royal Visit, Forfar, Scotland, 23 April 1941. Another detachment of Polish soldiers prepares to march past King George VI, Queen Elizabeth and General Sikorski. (AHA)

34. Churchill tanks, Scotland, early 1942. The Poles were supplied with 15 Infantry Tank Mk IV Churchill IIs. They were operated by the 65th Tank Battalion. They were unpopular with their crews who regarded them as unreliable and requiring excessive maintenance. The Churchill II was armed with a 2pdr main armament and only served in the training role. Here, a number of Churchills are lined up in a field, the one on the right has had part of its trackguards removed, possibly for maintenance. None of the vehicles appear to display any obvious markings, apart from a tank number on the lower front hull. (AHA)

35. Churchill tanks, Scotland, early 1942. Churchill IIs in the same bivouac as the previous photo. Here the crew appear to be conducting some basic maintenance, with one crewman working on the rear of the tank. Another rests on the open side hatch. (AHA)

36. Polish Infantry, Lanarkshire, Scotland, 1941. Polish infantrymen from I Polish Corps stand at ease on parade at a War Weapons Week event (localised raising of funds to support the war effort). All are wearing standard British Army battledress with 1937 webbing, with their gasmasks at the "ready position". Their helmets all carry the Polish national insignia of an eagle painted in yellow gas-detecting paint. In the first row, from left to right two of the four officers wear pistols in holsters on their left hip. The fifth and six soldiers are holding Thompson M1928 sub-machine guns with either the ammunition clip or drum removed. The seventh soldier holds a Bren light machine gun. The other soldiers appear to be carrying SMLE Mk III rifles. (AHA)

37. Rifle Range Practice, Fort William, Scotland, 7 May 1942. Polish soldiers practice firing the Mk III SMLE (Short, Magazine, Lee Enfield) the standard British Army rifle. On the left of the picture a British Army NCO small arms instructor stands ready to offer advice. For many Polish soldiers the Mk III SMLE would be the third rifle type they would have experienced in some three years. Those in the Polish Army in 1939 would have used the Mauser based *Karabinek wz.1929*. In France, 1939-40 soldiers would have probably been issued with Berthier 1916 rifles or the more modern *MAS Modèle 36*. Later in the war the Mk III would be replaced by the No 4 Mk I rifle, which the infantrymen of the 1st Polish Armoured Division would carry in Normandy. (Marta Piskorowska)

38. General Władysław Anders (1892-1970) Scotland, spring 1942. The General visits the 1st Polish Armoured Division. In 1939 he was a Cavalry Brigade commander and was taken prisoner by the Red Army. Following the German invasion of the Soviet Union in June 1941, he was released and was appointed by General Sikorski to command a new Polish Army to fight alongside the Soviets. Due to political and supply issues, Anders and his men were evacuated to Palestine where he formed the Polish II Corps which later fought in Italy. Post-war he remained in Britain, General Stanisław Maczek can be seen, wearing a traditional *Rogatywka* (garrison hat) standing fourth in line behind Anders. (AHA)

39. General Sikorski, Blairgowrie, Scotland, spring 1942. Inspection of 16th Tank Brigade, escorted, on his right, by the Brigade commander, Colonel Tadeusz Majewski, who as a subaltern, commanded a platoon of tanks at the battle of Korosten (now in the Ukraine) in 1920, during the Polish-Soviet War. In Normandy in 1944 he would command the 10th Armoured Cavalry Brigade. (AHA)

40. King Peter of Yugoslavia, Blairgowrie, Scotland, 1942. Escorted by General Sikorski (left) the exiled King Peter (second left) visits the Polish I Corps together with Wladyslaw Rackiewicz (1885-1947) President of the Republic of Poland 1939-47 (right). In the centre of the picture stands Colonel Franciszek Skibinski (1899-1991). A close associate of General Maczek before and during the war, he served as chief-of-staff for the 10th Armoured Cavalry Brigade from its formation in 1937 and during the 1939 campaign. Working with Maczek, first in France and later in Great Britain he held a number of key appointments and after the death in action on 20 August 1944 of Major Jan Maciejowski, commanding officer 10th Mounted Rifles, he briefly took over command of the regiment. For the rest of the campaign in North-West Europe he commanded first the 3rd Polish Infantry Brigade, August 1944 to January 1945, and from then the 10th Armoured Cavalry Brigade until July 1945. (AHA)

41. Lieutenant Colonel Zdzislaw Lubicz-Szydlowski Scotland, 1943. Commanding officer 9th Infantry Battalion (*9 Batalion Strzelcow)* inspects the guard, all of whom are equipped with Mk III Sten Guns. Commisioned in 1920 as an infantry Second Lieutenant he was severely wounded during the Battle of Warsaw. In July 1944 he was the commanding officer 9th Infantry Battalion in the 3rd Polish Infantry Brigade (*3 Brygada Strzelcow*). As the most senior officer on the *Maczuga* (Hill 262 North, Falaise Pocket) during the fighting 19-21 August 1944 he lacked a headquarters to direct a brigade-sized battlegroup and, also responsible for his own battalion's sector on the position, he had neither the time, nor the communications to directly exercise command, but was able to ensure effective co-operation between his fellow commanders on the *Maczuga*. In January 1945 he became second in command of the 3rd Polish Infantry Brigade for the rest of the war. He did not return to Poland. (PISM)

42. Crusader tanks, Scotland, 1942. Two Cruiser Mk VI Crusader Mk 1 from the 1st Armoured Regiment, 16th Armoured Brigade, 1st Polish Armoured Division have pulled off the road to shelter under some trees. The four-man crew tank taking advantage of the halt all wear berets rather than protective helmets. The vehicle is carrying a variety of markings. On the left hand front is the circle and wing symbol of the I Polish Corps. Just in front of the drivers position is the "PL" (Polish) nationality marking. Beneath the machine gun turret is the Arm of Service Number "072" indicating its subordination to the 1st Armoured Regiment. The armoured vehicle's "T" number is displayed at the bottom centre of the front plate. At this time the Crusader Mk 1, mounting a 2 pounder gun, was serving as the 8th Army's standard cruiser tank in North Africa, where combat experience often resulted in the Besa machine-gun turret (seen here mounted on the right of the tank) being removed and the space plated over. (PISM)

43. Crusader tank, 1942. A Cruiser Mk VI Crusader Mk III from the 10th Mounted Rifles, 10th Armoured Cavalry Brigade leads a column of Crusaders along a road. The turret crew appear to be wearing the 1940 Non-Crash Helmet Royal Tank Corps, second pattern with headphone wings later replaced by the improved RAC steel rimless helmet. The crewman on the left appears to be wearing black overalls. The tank prominently displays "A" Squadron markings on the turret. On the front of the tank is the red-white-red Royal Armoured Corps flash. Originally applied to tanks during the First World War, the practice of displaying this marking on tanks was revived for the early years of the war. On the front of the tank there are a number of markings. From the left is the bridge classification sign, the Arm of Service marking "51" for the 10th Mounted Rifles, on the right the "Winged Hussar" divisional insignia. The Mk III mounted a six pounder gun and was the last gun-armed Crusader to see action, serving with the 1st and 8th Armies in North Africa. (PISM)

44. Scotland, 1942. A Polish soldier attempts to lighten the mood. Judging by the expressions on the faces of his comrades, with limited success. The soldiers are probably on a training march rather than an exercise. They do not appear to be carrying gas masks or steel helmets. However they are now fully equipped with British Army uniforms, webbing and equipment. They carry SMLE rifles. They are however wearing their beret and badges in the Polish style. Note that the rank insignia is still worn to the left of the centrally positioned national eagle cap badge, prior to change in early 1943 to directly under the eagle. (AHA)

NACZELNY WÓDZ I MINISTER SPRAW WOJSKOWYCH

CENTRALNA KOMISJA REGULAMINOWA

O.29
——
1942

INSTRUKCJA

O SPOSOBIE NOSZENIA

OPORZĄDZENIA

Wielka Brytania
1942

45-49. Polish Military Instructional Booklet. *Instrukcja O Sposobre Noszenia Oporzadzenia, 1942.* Published by the Polish Military Authorities in the United Kingdom this booklet explains how to assemble and wear their British Army issue webbing, pouches and kit. By 1941 most of the free Allied governments in London had established their own armed forces in exile. By necessity all were issued with British Army uniforms and weapons, but all took advantage, where possible, to include distinctive badges and symbols from their own military traditions, as shown in these drawings of a Polish soldier who, although wearing British uniform, still wears his own national insignia on headgear, collar and shoulder straps. (AHA)

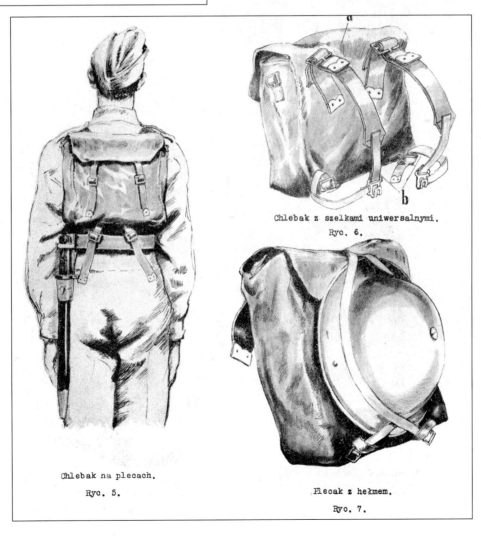

Chlebak na plecach.
Ryc. 5.

Chlebak z szelkami uniwersalnymi.
Ryc. 6.

Plecak z hełmem.
Ryc. 7.

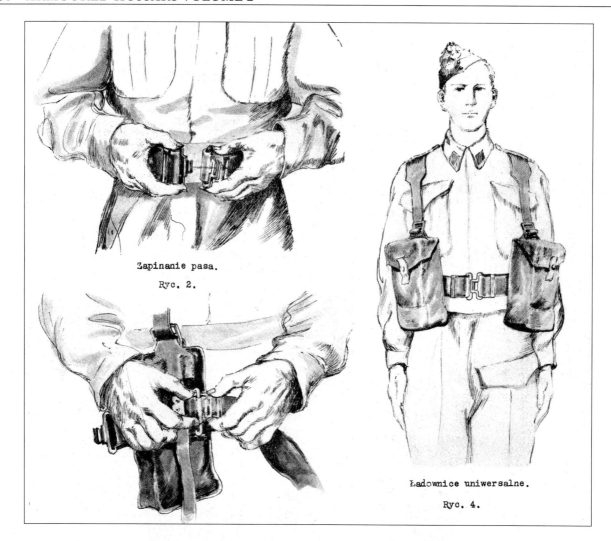

Zapinanie pasa.

Ryc. 2.

Ładownice uniwersalne.

Ryc. 4.

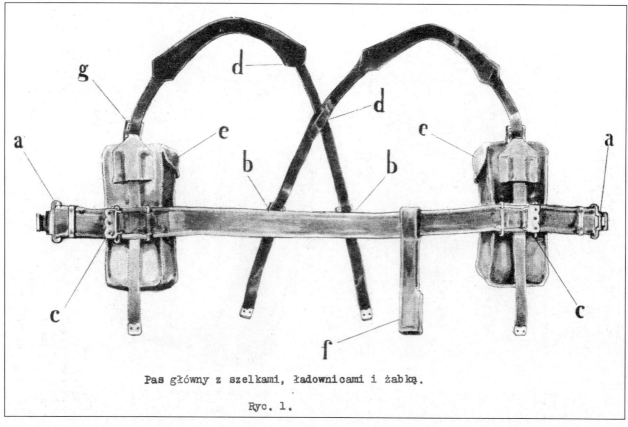

Pas główny z szelkami, ładownicami i żabką.

Ryc. 1.

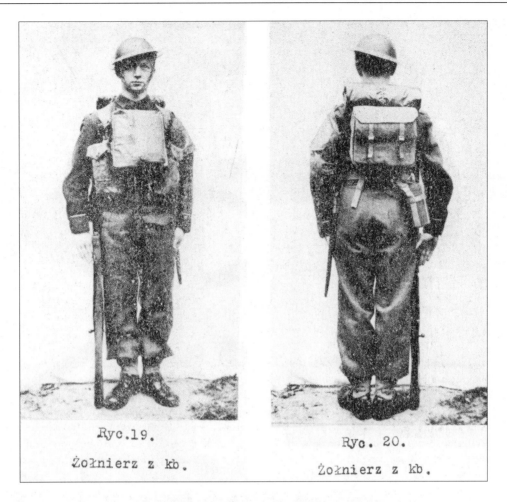

Ryc.19.

Żołnierz z kb.

Ryc. 20.

Żołnierz z kb.

50. Patrol, Scotland circa 1942-43. Soldiers from an Armoured Regiment, with their distinctive British tank crew helmets embossed with the Polish National Eagle emblem, patrol on guard though an unidentified Scottish-English border town. Note Post Office Telephone Box top right and also the white-painted stripes on the lamppost as part of the black-out regulations. (AHA)

51. Armoured Regiment briefing, Scotland, 1943. Tank crewmen parade wearing a mixture of uniforms. Some, including the soldier front left, are wearing the black two-piece working dress introduced for the Royal Tank Corps in 1935 and largely phased out of use by the British Army by late 1941. However, this uniform appears to have been enthusiastically adopted by Polish Officers from surplus stocks and is seen sporadically worn until embarkation for Normandy (see photo 64). The others are wearing standard khaki drill coveralls. All are wearing their revolvers in the holsters on the left. Earlier in the war a holster was worn strapped to the right thigh for ease of access and to avoid catching on various parts of the interior fittings of the tank. All are wearing the beret in the Polish style, pulled to the rear, rather than to the side, as in the British Army. (PISM)

52. 1st Armoured Regiment, 10th Armoured Cavalry Brigade, Aldershot, June 1944. Sherman V tanks lined up after exercise following a period of intense pre-invasion training. Note the markings on the foreground tank which has, on its front, side the old Royal Armoured Corps red-white-red flash (see photo 43). Also note the "diamond" HQ Squadron marking seen on the turret of the first and third tanks, which is also missing its left side "sandskirt" and front mudguard which were often easily damaged and removed in operational condition. However note the last Sherman in the row still has them intact and that this particular vehicle is having its barrel cleaned (see photo 70). (PISM)

TABLICA 3.

WIDOK Z PRZODU

53-56. Sherman V Manual. 1944. As the Poles were using the same equipment, British Army training and instructional material had to be provided and translated into Polish, from a booklet on the Sherman. These images show the front, rear, side and overhead exterior profile of the tank. (AHA).

TABLICA 4.

WIDOK Z TYŁU

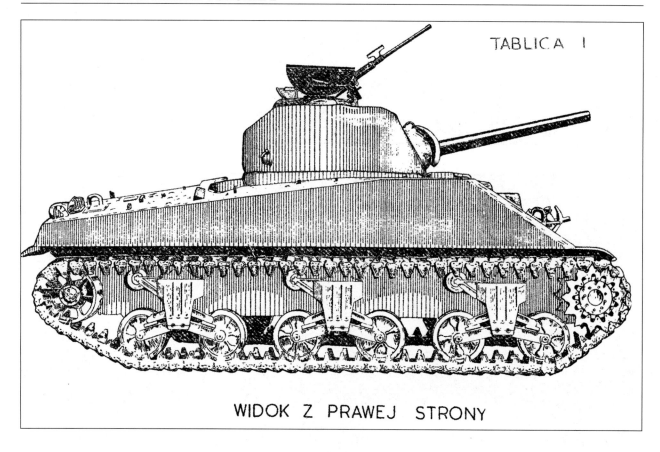

TABLICA 1

WIDOK Z PRAWEJ STRONY

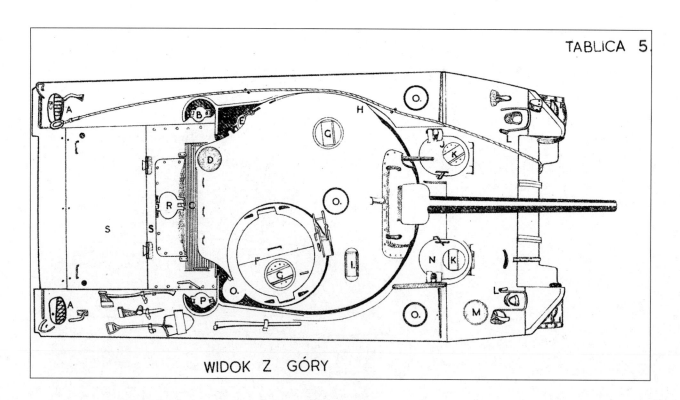

TABLICA 5.

WIDOK Z GÓRY

T A B L I C A   6.

1. Dźwignie kierownicze
2. K.m. przedni (w kadłubie)
3. Siedzenie kierowcy
5. Właz kierowcy
6. Działo 75 mm
7. Ucho do dźwigania wieży
8. Otwór wentylacyjny
9. Kopułka wieży
10. Peryskop dowódcy
12. Siedzenie w wieży
13. Siedzenie celowniczego
14. Siedzenie w koszu w wieży
15. Wieża
16. Filtr powietrza
17. Klapa wlewu chłodnicy wody
18. Przewód zasysanego powietrza
19. Zespół silnikowy
20. Rura wydechowa
21. Koło napinające
22. Pompka wodna (w układzie o jednej pompce wodnej)
23. Chłodnica wody
24. Prądnica główna (w układzie o jednej pompce wodne
25. Tylny wał kardanowy
26. Kosz wieży
27. Łącznica obrotowa
28. Przedni wał kardanowy
29. Wózek zawieszenia
30. Skrzynka przekładniowa biegów
31. Koło napędzające gąsienicę.

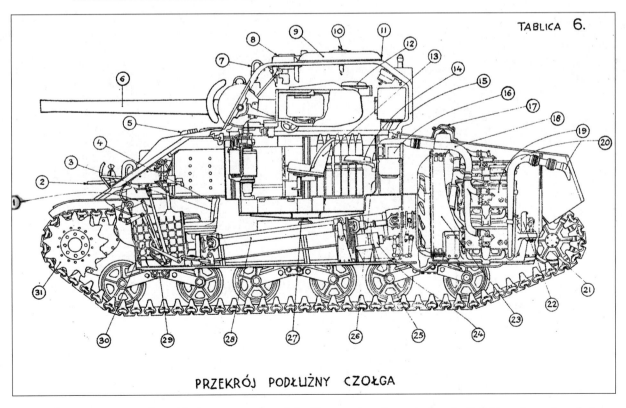

TABLICA 6.

PRZEKRÓJ PODŁUŻNY CZOŁGA

57-58. Sherman V Manual, 1944. A cut-away plan of the Sherman interior and a key (in Polish) to the various fittings and equipment indicated. (AHA)

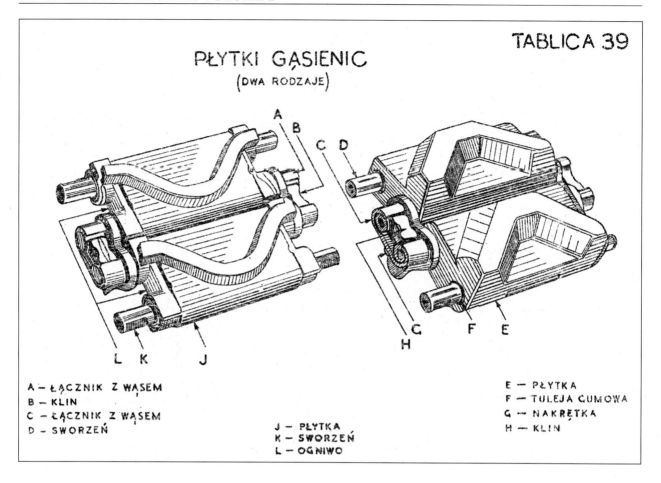

PŁYTKI GĄSIENIC
(DWA RODZAJE)

TABLICA 39

A — ŁĄCZNIK Z WĄSEM
B — KLIN
C — ŁĄCZNIK Z WĄSEM
D — SWORZEŃ

J — PŁYTKA
K — SWORZEŃ
L — OGNIWO

E — PŁYTKA
F — TULEJA GUMOWA
G — NAKRĘTKA
H — KLIN

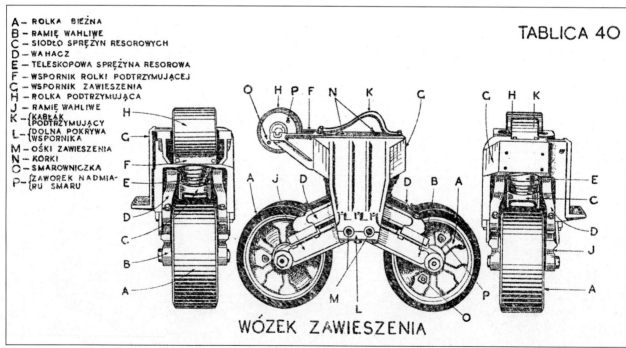

TABLICA 40

A — ROLKA BIEŻNA
B — RAMIĘ WAHLIWE
C — SIODŁO SPRĘŻYN RESOROWYCH
D — WAHACZ
E — TELESKOPOWA SPRĘŻYNA RESOROWA
F — WSPORNIK ROLKI PODTRZYMUJĄCEJ
G — WSPORNIK ZAWIESZENIA
H — ROLKA PODTRZYMUJĄCA
J — RAMIĘ WAHLIWE
K — {KABŁĄK PODTRZYMUJĄCY
L — {DOLNA POKRYWA WSPORNIKA
M — OŚKI ZAWIESZENIA
N — KORKI
O — SMAROWNICZKA
P — {ZAWOREK NADMIA- RU SMARU

WÓZEK ZAWIESZENIA

59-60. Sherman V Manual, 1944. Diagram showing detail of the tracks and road-wheels. (AHA)

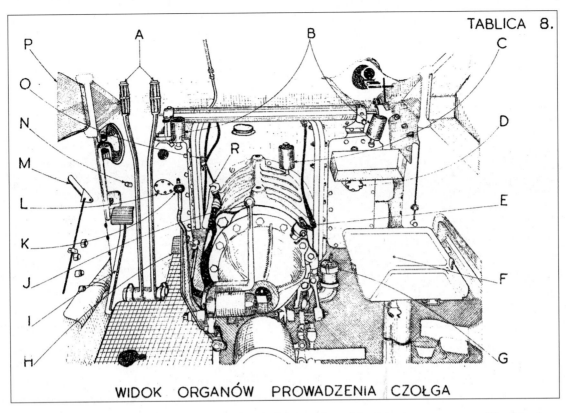

61. Sherman V Manual, 1944. Diagram showing detail of the interior of the driver's compartment. The driver's seat is on the left and the assistant driver's position is on the right. Between them is the transmission. (AHA)

62. Second Armoured Regiment training exercise, Yorkshire, England, 1944 (sequential photos 62-64). Sherman V tanks move across an open field on exercise. The tank to the left is leading a column consisting of a Valentine bridge-layer followed by a couple of M5 half-tracks. The Sherman on the right is probably leading a similar grouping. The tank on the left carries a square symbol on its turret indicating that that this troop belongs to the tank regiment's "B" squadron. Both Shermans carry very prominent Allied White-Star recognition stars on their sides. Operational experience would come to modify the size and placement of this symbol, which would be reduced in size, or obscured to prevent it being used as an aiming mark by enemy gunners. The Sherman on the left mounts a 0.50 calibre Browning heavy machine gun. Primarily intended as defence against low-flying aircraft it could also be deadly effective against un-armoured ground targets. (PISM)

63. Second Armoured Regiment training exercise, Yorkshire, England, 1944. Polish tanks with Valentine bridge-laying tanks move forward during an exercise. Their presence probably indicates that obstacle crossing drills are being practiced. The Valentine bridge-layer could deploy a Class 30 Bridge, with a length of 34 feet with a width of 9 1/2 feet, able to carry a 30 ton load. Another photographer recording the exercise can be seen kneeling on the ground between the leading Fireflys. (PISM)

64. Second Armoured Regiment training exercise, Yorkshire, England, 1944. Shermans move forward during the same exercise shown in photo 63. The four Shermans are from two different squadrons. The Firefly in the left foreground prominently carries the "triangle' symbol of "A" squadron of the 2nd Armoured Regiment and is the right hand Firefly seen in the centre of the preceding image. The two other Shermans and Firefly are probably from the same regiment's "B" squadron (the "square" symbol on the turret of the leading tank). All the tanks prominently carry White-Star recognition markings on their hull, which would usually be obscured following combat experience in Normandy. All the vehicles carry an encircled allied White-Star recognition marking on their rear decks. All tanks mount 0.50 calibre heavy machine guns. Note the crews of the two leading tanks appear to be still wearing the former Royal Tank Corps black two-piece working dress subsequently enthusiastically adopted by Polish Officers (see photo 51). (PISM)

65. **First Anti-Tank Artillery Regiment M10/Achilles, Yorkshire, England, 1944**. A M10/Achilles on exercise. Each British, Polish and Canadian armoured division had an anti-tank regiment with a total of 24 × M10/Achilles tank destroyers. The M10, was originally fitted with a 3 inch (76mm) gun, but whose performance proved not significantly superior to the standard Sherman's 75mm gun. As a result the British Army modified some of these vehicles to mount the 17 pounder and this modification was known as the "Achilles" (its distinctive feature was the counter-weight mounted on the gun, immediately behind the muzzle-brake). Its particular weakness was its open topped turret, which made its crew to small arms fire and shrapnel. The crew of this particular vehicle are wearing the US Army issue "Rawlings" M38 Tanker Helmet (based on a pre-war football helmet), as often these came with the vehicle on delivery from the United States. (PISM)

66. Firefly, Yorkshire, England, 1944. A Firefly moves across a field during an exercise. The Firefly was the name given to a British modification, felt unnecessary by the US Army, of the Sherman V. It had been adapted to take the powerful High Velocity (HV) 17 pounder anti-tank gun, intended to improve the capability of British armour to deal with anticipated German armour threats that would be faced after D-Day. This photo shows the distinctive long gun, and the extension to the rear of the turret to provide space for the considerable recoil of the gun and to accommodate the vehicle's radio. As supply of these vehicles was limited, issue was usually on the scale of one per platoon. (PISM)

67. Second Field Artillery Regiment, Yorkshire, England, 1944. Gunners prepare to fire a 25 pounder gun-howitzer, (with a rate of fire of five rounds a minute) during a pre-D-Day exercise. The gun is concealed beneath camouflage netting. Another similar position, part of the same battery (eight guns), can be seen in the left background. The 25 pounder was one of the outstanding artillery pieces of the war and provided divisional level artillery support throughout the British Army and all British equipped allied armies. With a maximum range of 13,400 yards it could fire a variety of ammunition types, including armour-piercing, which had proved particularly valuable during the campaign in North Africa 1941-42. Alongside the gun can be seen its associated ammunition trailer containing 32 rounds in trays (with two rounds per tray), one of which can be seen open with a gunner about to extract a round. Missing is the circular metal firing platform usually carried beneath the gun's trail that could be lowered to the ground before the gun came into action. Once mounted on the platform the gun could be swiftly traversed through 360 degrees. With the gun about to fire the foreground gunner has turned away, after ramming the round into the breech. The total gun detachment was six. A Morris Quad tractor (one of which can be seen in photo 68) towed both gun and trailer. Each armoured division had two Field Artillery Regiments. One equipped with 24 × towed 25 pounders, the other with 24 Sexton 25 pounder self-propelled guns. (PISM)

68. First Anti-Tank Artillery Regiment, Yorkshire, England, 1944. Gunners prepare to limber up a 17 pounder anti-tank gun, the most effective anti-tank gun in service with British, Canadian and Polish anti-tank regiments in Normandy, with a maximum range of 10,000 yards. Before going into action the trails would have been separated to provide a stable firing platform and the spades at each end would have been dug-in. It was towed, either by a Morris Quad (seen here) or M5 half-track. Like other British and Canadian armoured divisions, the Polish 1st Antitank Artillery Regiment deployed a total of 24 × towed 17 pounders and 24 × self-propelled M10/Achilles. Because of its high level of effectiveness against German armour it was also modified for use in the Sherman Firefly, see photo 66. (PISM)

69. Stuart Mk V, Kirkcudbright range, Scotland spring 1944 (sequential photos 69-72). Stuart Mk V light tanks line up for practice on the firing ranges. The American-built Stuart first saw action with the British 8th Army in North Africa in 1941, where it earned the nickname "Honey" due to its high reliability and standards of construction, but by 1944 it was obsolete. Each Armoured Regiment, and the Armoured Reconnaissance Regiment, had a reconnaissance platoon of 11 of these vehicles. It was armed with a 37mm gun. (AHA)

70. Stuart Mk V, Kirkcudbright range, Scotland spring 1944. Tank crews carry out maintenance on their Stuart Mk V light tank after practice on the firing ranges. A long barrel rod is used by crewmen to clean the rifling within the barrel which was necessary daily to ensure accuracy by preventing the build-up of dirt. Another crewman is returning the bow-mounted Browning 1919 0.30 calibre machine gun to its mounting inside the hill after cleaning. (AHA)

71. Kirkcudbright range, Scotland Spring 1944. Crew prepare to move off with Sergeant Jan Pirog seen leaning out of the turret, minus headphones. Pirog served in the 1st Anti-Tank Artillery Regiment and was attached to the 10th Mounted Rifle Regiment, the Division's armoured reconnaissance regiment.(AHA)

72. Kirkcudbright range. Scotland Spring 1944. A Stuart Mk V moves off the range area, which was located on the northern coastline of the Solway Firth in Dumfries and Galloway. (AHA)

73. General Montgomery, Divisional inspection, Kelso, Scotland, 13 April 1944. "Monty" as he was nicknamed, addresses the officers and men of the 1st Polish Armoured Division, after their mobilization on 19 March 1944. In his role of Commander 21st Army Group, he regularly visited all the units under his command, both to assess their readiness and to give inspiration addresses to the men. His most famous speech included "We will go forward together, you and I, to kill the Germans", used to motivate the largely untried Allied Army Group. Adopting an informal style he was one of the first senior officers to wear battledress and often appeared in just a sweater and trousers topped with his famous beret adorned with a Royal Tank Corps cap badge in addition to his General Officer's badge (see photo 74). Unfortunately the Poles, who had a more formal military tradition in these matters, were not particularly enamored by this approach and were more impressed by the appearance of General Eisenhower, Supreme Allied Commander of the Allied Expeditionary Force for the invasion of Europe, when he visited the division.(AHA)

74. Major Koszutski, 2nd Armoured Regiment, Kelso, Scotland, 13 April 1944. Left to right: Major Stanisław Pawel Koszutski (1903-82) Commander Second Armoured Regiment, General Stanisław Maczek (1892-1994), General Montgomery (note on his shoulder he wears the formation badge of 21st Army Group) and Colonel Tadeusz Majewski, commander of the 10th Armoured Cavalry Brigade. An artilleryman between the wars he also served in the Polish Military Geographical Institute. At the outbreak of war in 1939 Koszutski served as Quartermaster with the Wolynska Cavalry Brigade and later with the General Anders Operational Cavalry Group. Captured by the Soviets he was able to escape, first to France, where he attended the *Ecole de Guerre* and then to Great Britain where he became operations officer to the 10th Armoured Cavalry Brigade and Head of Training. In 1942 he became commanding officer of the 2nd Armoured Regiment (*2 Pulk Pancerny*). Promoted Lieutenant Colonel in March 1944 he led his Regiment into Normandy and from then to the end of April 1945. He did not return to Poland, exiled first to Great Britain and eventually migrating to Brazil, where he lived for the rest of his life. (AHA)

75. Major Kanski, 24th Lancer Regiment, Kelso, Scotland, 13 April 1944. Left to right: Major Jan Witold Kanski (1898-1944) Commander 24th Lancer (*Pulk Uhlan*) Regiment, Lieutenant General Janus Gluchowski, Commander in Chief Polish Army Forces in England (excluding the 1st Polish Independent Parachute Brigade which reported directly to the Government in Exile) General Maczek, General Montgomery, Lieutenant General Jozef Zajac, Inspector of Training, Polish Armed Forces in the West, and Colonel Tadeusz Majewski. Kanski was a cavalryman, most of his service was with the *24 Pulk Ulanow*, both before and during the war. During the 1939 campaign he commanded the Regiment's 3rd Squadron. He was interned in Hungary 1939-40 but was able to make his way first to France where he rejoined the regiment. Escaping to Great Britain he served as Regimental Adjutant 1941-1942. In August 1942 he was appointed Second in Command and in November 1943 its Commanding Officer. He lead the 24th Uhlans into action in Normandy during TOTALIZE and TRACTABLE. He was mortally wounded at Jort, on 16 August 1944, during an artillery barrage and died in hospital 29 August 1944. On the 25 November 1944, he was posthumously promoted to Lieutenant Colonel.(AHA)

76. **Major Stefanowicz, 1st Armoured Regiment, Kelso, Scotland, 13 April 1944**. Left to right: Major Aleksander Stefanowicz (1900-85), General Maczek, General Montgomery and Colonel Tadeusz Majewski. Stefanowicz served in a cavalry regiment during the '1920' Polish-Soviet war. In 1921 he joined the 1st Tank Regiment in Lodz as a platoon commander. For the rest of his pre-war service he was involved in the study of, and instruction in, armoured warfare and vehicles. He attended the French *Le ecole de application de Chars de Combat* at Versailles 1924-25. From May 1931 to 1st March 1932 he was travelling abroad "off active duty". On his return he produced a paper for the Centre for Armoured Weapons Studies. As an assistant military attaché in Lisbon he observed developments in armoured vehicles and warfare during the Spanish Civil War (1937-39) and then joined the Polish General Staff's Department II (Military Intelligence).

He escaped to France and in May 1940 was posted to the 10th Armoured Cavalry Regiment as adjutant to General Maczek. After the fall of France he made his way to Great Britain and in June 1942 he was appointed second in command of the 66th Tank Battalion (later the 2nd Armoured Regiment). In November 1943 he became commanding officer of the 1st Armoured Regiment (*1 Pulk Pancerny*) which he led into action in Normandy. Promoted Lieutenant Colonel on 7 September 1944 he continued to command his regiment until 1947. He did not return to Poland and was involved in the Polish Repatriation and Resettlement Corps. He emigrated to Canada where he lived for the rest of his life.

In early 1944 Major Stefanowicz received the following report after the visit of his unit, 1st Armoured Regiment, to Kirkcudbright ranges. Official Report (Abridged version) Armoured Fighting Vehicles Range, Kirkcudbright, Scotland, 25 Feb 1944.
To: Commanding Officer 1st Polish Armoured Regiment. Report on Units firing 18th to 21st February 1944. BATTLE PRACTICE: The general standard is very good, Gunners are quick to shoot and accurate. Commanders are very quick to spot targets and to let their Gunners on. H.E. (High Explosive). Fire is quickly put down and is effective but very often more tanks are used than is necessary on one target, it is generally quicker and more effective to use one tank against one target. A.P. (Armour Piercing). This is excellent. The accurate observation of Commanders, the exact corrections they give and the good eye of the Gunner, all result in the target being hit and being hit quickly. BROWNING MACHINE GUNS: Guns were well used and the shooting on the move with them was good. Gunners must learn not to fire very long bursts as the barrels will not stand up to it. REECE TROOP: Considering that this troop had very little previous experience with the Honey tank they have done very well. Gunners and Commanders are very keen and the shooting has improved greatly during the three days they have been here. 37-mm. SHOOTING: This was sound but the Gunners still need more practice, especially on moving targets. MAINTENANCE OF GUNNERY EQUIPMENT AND AMMUNITION: All crews know the gunnery equipment well and are thorough in it's maintenance. They keep the ammunition clean and serviceable. In conclusion I would like to say that I consider the Regiment has put up a very good performance indeed during its visit here. Officer I.G. Kirkcudbright. (AHA)

77. Divisional inspection, **Kelso, Scotland, 13 April 1944**. General Montgomery with General Stanisław Maczek (1892-1994), General Officer Commanding, 1st Polish Armoured Division (*1. Dywizja Pancerna*). In 1939, as Colonel Maczek commanding 10th Armoured Cavalry Brigade (*10. Brygada Kawalerii Pancernej*) he was the first allied commander of an armoured formation to lead it into action against the Germany's new *Panzer* divisions. In February 1942 he was appointed commander of the 1st Polish Armoured Division and was to lead it for the rest of the war. Afterwards he became an exile in the United Kingdom. He was laid to rest in the Polish military cemetery in Breda, Holland, the site of one of his Division's most impressive achievements, outflanking the German opposition and liberating the town with minimal structural damage and few civilian losses, alongside those he led in battle.(AHA)

Part II
Normandy, 6 June 1944–7 August 1944

By late 1943 it was obvious to the Western Allies that to make a decisive contribution to the final defeat of Nazi Germany it would be necessary for them to launch a massive invasion at some point along the French Coast and then advance across North-West Europe with as strong as force as could be mustered, to force the surrender of Nazi Germany by the destruction of its armed forces in the West. By 1944 Normandy had been selected as the most suitable landing area. The beaches were suitable for assault, and the area would be in the range of Allied air cover operating from the United Kingdom. In comparison with the heavily fortified Pas de Calais, the German defences in Normandy were much less formidable and thus more likely to be quickly overcome. The capture of nearby Cherbourg would provide the invasion force with a major port for supplies. The planned timing of early summer promised good weather and Stalin had promised to co-ordinate the start of the Red Army's summer offensive with the landings. In fact Operation *BAGRATION* would be launched on 22 June (the third anniversary of Operation *Barbarossa*).

On 6 June 1944 British, American and Canadian forces fought their way ashore in the opening phase of the Battle for Normandy. Over the next few weeks the Allied armies would engage their opponents in a serious of ferocious battles.

In some of these, infantry casualties in 2nd British Army ran at a higher level than some of the battles on the Western Front during the First World War. The scale of German resistance was ferocious. On the Eastern flank the British 2nd Army fought a prolonged campaign to capture the key objective of Caen, which it had hoped to seize on D-Day. The city and the open country to the south was viewed as the linchpin of the eastern sector of the front and it was on this point, according to Montgomery's plan that the whole Allied front would pivot during the breakout phase. Similarly the Germans regarded Caen as vital to the German position in Normandy, and concentrated their armoured forces in its defence.

To the West, aided by the German concentration on defending Caen US forces had cleared the Contentin Peninsula and captured the port of Cherbourg (Montgomery had declared to General Bradley, the American commander 'Caen is the key to Cherbourg'). However its defenders had conducted such a comprehensive demolition programme of the port facilities that although the German garrison surrendered on 29 June, it was not until the middle of August that limited port operations could resume.

After a series of intense and prolonged battles, in operations such as EPSOM, JUPITER, and CHARNWOOD the northern part of Caen was captured on 9 July 1944. This was followed by Operation GOODWOOD an attack southwards by three armoured divisions on 18 July. The offensive achieved only a limited success. Although there was no breakthrough, the mass of German amour still remained fixed facing the British and Canadians, with only three *Panzer/Panzergrenadier* divisions opposing the Americans.

In the meantime US forces had pushed through the dense *bocage.* These ancient small fields surrounded by dense, long established hedges restricted forward movement for both men and vehicles and provided excellent ambush and defence positions for German machine-guns and anti-tank weapons. After more heavy fighting the Americans captured the strategic town of St Lo on 24 July.

The 1st Polish and 4th Canadian Armoured (which deployed to Normandy at the same time) were the last armoured divisions Montgomery's 21st Army Group would receive as reinforcements until 1945. The Poles and Canadians joined the Guards, 7th, and 11th Armoured Divisions already in action. Additionally there was the 79th Armoured Division with its various specialist armoured vehicles, three Independent Tank Brigades; 6th Guards, 31st and 34th with Churchill Infantry Support Tanks and also five Independent Armoured Brigades; 2nd Canadian, 4th , 8th , 27th and 33rd with Sherman tanks. The struggles between the British and German armoured formations in Normandy was the most intense since that experienced in the North African Campaign, 1941-43. During this period armoured units, their commanders and soldiers had both encountered problems, sought solutions and learnt lessons that the Poles would both experience and adjust to when they entered combat in August.

The British armoured division's role in battle was to act offensively, break through enemy defences and then exploit any success by pursuit. However in the fighting following D-Day British armoured divisions had not been able to fully carry out this role due to a variety of factors such as terrain, quality of the opposing forces, the technical balance between both sides and tactical, doctrinal and organisational factors.

The allies expected that once they had judged the Allied landings to have been successful, the Germans would fall back into the French interior and fight a mobile battle between the Seine and the Loire, out of range of the effects of Allied naval gunfire, using the mobile tactics they were using on the Eastern Front, taking advantage of the accuracy and long range of their tank and anti-tank guns. However Hitler had ordered his forces to hold fast and the *bocage,* which the Allies assumed would be quickly left behind, became the main battleground. One that particular favoured the defender who was able to exploit the thick hedgerows, small fields and thick-walled stoned cottages and farms to his advantage. All this provided excellent cover for concealed and camouflaged tanks, self-propelled guns, anti-tank guns and infantry with man-portable anti-tank weapons such as the *Panzerfaust* and *Panzerschrek.* Vehicle navigation was difficult and infantry support essential, but this involved heavy casualties.

German defences were also found to be organised to a greater depth than had been encountered before. It was therefore possible to achieve break-ins, but very difficult to achieve breakthroughs through enemy positions. Often it was found that although supporting artillery bombardments and bombing raids seriously damaged forward enemy positions those to the rear were untouched.

Also in Normandy the British Army, and its allies, were encountering the largest and most powerful concentration of German forces they had faced since 1940.

Although the coastal defence divisions and some of the less mobile infantry divisions were of poor quality, the core component of the German defences were the *Panzer* divisions of the German Army (*Heer*) and the *Waffen-SS*. Although by the end of July two (and a weaker *Panzergrenadier* division) had been redeployed to face the Americans, three from the *Heer* and four of the *Waffen-SS*'s total of seven Panzer were currently still opposing the British and Canadians together with the only three Tiger heavy tank battalions deployed in the West. All these were led by determined commanders, officers and NCOs many of who had wide combat experience from fighting the Red Army on the Eastern front. *Waffen-SS* troops proving particularly effective (and sometimes brutal) battlefield opponents.

Tank combat since D-Day had revealed certain deficiencies in the quality of allied armour, which was certainly felt by some of their crews. The Sherman was still able to hold its own against the up-armoured and up-gunned versions of the PzKw IV (albeit with some difficulty), and the limited-traverse StuG III *Sturmgeschutz* (Assault Gun) which would provide the majority of the enemy armour types encountered in Normandy. The Sherman enjoyed the advantage of a high-rate of fire and a faster speed of turret traverse compared to its German opponents.

However, the Sherman was proving particularly vulnerable to the powerful German "big cats" with their powerful High Velocity (HV) weapons, the heavy PzKw VI Tiger tank with the 88mm KwK (*KampfwagenKanone*) 36 and medium PzKw V Panther with a 75mm KwK 42 tank gun. In encounters with these enemy tanks, Sherman crews were at a serious disadvantage as both German types could destroy a Sherman well beyond the effective range of its own 75mm MV gun. The Sherman was also regarded as being vulnerable to catching fire when hit and penetrated. This was believed to be the fault of the tank's petrol engine. This earned the Sherman the nickname of "Ronson" (after the advert for the popular brand of cigarette lighter with its slogan of "lights every time") from the British Army, and that of "Tommy-Cooker" from the Germans. In fact it seems the culprit was the Sherman's own ammunition. This was stored in the side sponsons of the tank and was inadequately protected. To protect the sides of the tank, extra applique sheets of armour were applied, but later investigations showed this measure to be useless, merely providing German tank and, anti-tank gunners with visible aiming marks. A remedy was achieved by the introduction of improved systems of ammunition storage.

Normandy was the first time the Firefly went into action and was the most powerfully armed tank in the Allied invasion force and capable of dealing with all types of German armour encountered. It was a Firefly, either from the Northamptonshire Yeomanry, the Canadian Sherbrooke Fusiliers or 144 Royal Armoured Corps, that knocked out the Tiger of *Waffen-SS* "tank ace" *Hauptsturmfuhrer* Michael Wittman on 8 August, the opening day of Operation TOTALIZE. Its effectiveness was only limited by the relatively small numbers available. On 11 June there were 84 Fireflys in service in Normandy, 149 by the end of the month, and 235 by the end of July.

As well as tanks the Germans were deploying increasing numbers of self-propelled anti-tank guns, such as the *Marder III Sd.Kfz.139*, based on the obsolete hull of an early war Czech designed tank, on which was mounted the powerful Pak 40, the standard German 75mm anti-tank gun, which could knock out all the Allied armour types encountered. While their usually open top made them vulnerable to artillery, they could quickly relocate after firing from hidden or camouflaged ambush positions.

In combat since D-Day the German defenders consistently demonstrated a high level of tactical skill. Allied advances were usually immediately faced by rapidly organised counter-attacks as German troops attempted to re-take their lost positions before adequate defences could be organised.

There were also doubts amongst commanders whether the structure of the armoured division was suitable for the type of combat they were encountering, with a shortage of infantry in the motor battalions and the difficulties of armour-infantry co-operation with the armoured division's separate infantry brigade. This was in contrast to the German *kampfgruppe*, an *ad hoc* military formation, usually comprising a combination of all-arms of about battalion strength (not necessarily from the same unit), but could be larger, or smaller, if required. *Kampfgruppen* were usually assembled for a specific task, but could stay in existence for some time. They were given the name of the senior officer in command.

However British tank crews and their commanders were learning to deal with these problems. It was found that once a successful attack had been made, it was important to immediately organise the position for anti-tank defence with guns and tanks to deal with the inevitable German counter-attacks. Also considerable artillery resources were available. In Normandy, British, Polish and Canadian commanders could call upon some 4,500 guns in support. If the defence of recently captured ground could be quickly organised, with tanks and self-propelled artillery rapidly brought up to reinforce the position and artillery support organised German counter attacks could not only be held but also be subjected to devastating bombardment. The Germans, who unlike the allies received no regular reinforcements of men or equipment, were steadily being destroyed in a violent battle of attrition.

This was the nature of the battlefield environment in which the 1st Polish Armoured Division would soon be engaged.

On 25 July 1944, the US forces in Normandy, now reinforced by the arrival of General George Patton's 3rd US Army, launched Operation COBRA, the intended break-through the German lines. After an uncertain start COBRA gathered speed as its spearheads advanced towards Brittany. There was the danger that faced with this threat the Germans might redeploy some of their armoured divisions facing the British and Canadians to counter the American advance.

To prevent this Montgomery therefore ordered an attack by 2nd British Army to support the American advance by striking into an area currently lightly held by the Germans, immediately on the left flank of the US 1st Army. In three days the 76,000 men and 13,500 vehicles of four British divisions were relocated to their new positions and Operation BLUCOAT was launched on 30 July 1944. To maintain pressure on the German defenders south of Caen the newly activated 1st Canadian Army, under the command of Lieutenant General H.D.G."Harry" Crerar was ordered to push towards Falaise.

On 1 August there was a major change to the Allied Command structure. Following the reinforcement of Allied forces since D-Day, 21st Army Group was now divided into two. The British-Canadian component retained the 21st Army Group title, while the US Forces were re-organised into the 12th Army Group under the command of General Bradley. Each Army Group now consisted of two subordinate armies. Under command of 21st Army Group were 1st Canadian Army and 2nd British Army. Under command of 12 Army Group were the existing 1st US Army and the newly arrived 3rd US Army. (However General Montgomery remained in operational command of both Army Groups, and would continue do so until General Eisenhower's SHAEF became operational on 1 September).

On 7 August, 1st Canadian Army Rear HQ reported the 1st Polish Armoured Division complete with its full complement of vehicles and equipment, 129 Sherman V tanks, 25 Sherman VC (the official designation for the Firefly), 33 Stuarts and 59 Cromwells, 13,000 men and over 4,000 vehicles. The 1st Polish Armoured Division was now ready for combat.

At 02.30 on 8 August 1944 the 1st Polish Armoured Division, under command of II Canadian Corps began moving from Bayeux to its assembly areas south of Caen to take part in its first combat operation in World War II. From then until 21 August, the division would experience a dramatic baptism of fire in one of the most significant armoured engagements of the war as it played a key role in the final battles of the Normandy campaign culminating in a desperate struggle on the slopes of Mont Ormel and in the streets of the nearby small town of Chambois.

Part III
TOTALIZE and TRACTABLE
8–16 August 1944

by Ken Tout

For the 1st Polish Armoured Division, 7 August 1944 signalled the end of a long and terrible odyssey leading to this time of vengeance. Numbers of the tank crews had first entered action against the German army in September 1939. Many had endured retreat against vastly superior forces (Soviet as well as Nazi), been evacuated, and interned, fighting again in France and trained in what must have seemed everlasting exile in Scotland. Now, at long last, the division had landed in Normandy only a day or two ago. From its laager near Bayeux it was moving across country towards its first day of action as a unit. If the division's history was extraordinary so was the Operation in which it was about to take a leading part: TOTALIZE.

The division traced its origins back to the 1937 unit, the 10th Armoured Cavalry Brigade which had fought from the beginning of the war under the command of the then Colonel Stanislaw Maczek. During 1942 and 1943 in Scotland the unit was enlarged into an armoured division, now commanded by the same Stanislaw Maczek. One of the Polish units, 24th *Uhlans*, estimated that 80% of its personnel had been evacuated or found their way directly from Poland. The remainder came from a variety of countries, some as remote as Argentina and Lithuania. Some 20% of the soldiers had fought in Poland in September 1939 and 30% had fought in France around the time of Dunkirk. The division therefore had considerable battle experience compared with the not untypical British tank regiment through which it passed at Saint Aignan which had less than two months front line experience.

In spite of Montgomery's intention to capture Caen on D-Day itself, 6 June, it had taken the Allies a month to liberate that city. The 2nd British and 1st Canadian Armies then found themselves confronted by a long, gentle ridge, around Bourguebus and Verrieres. Along this vista of woods, solid stone farms, and sunken roads the Germans with their more powerful guns were ensconced, able to see every Allied move on the plain below. Another month went by including Operation GOODWOOD, termed 'The Death Ride of the Armoured Divisions' when a drive by almost 800 tanks still failed to do more than obtain a lodgement some way up the long slope.

The poisoned chalice of assaulting the ridge was handed to Lieutenant General Guy Simonds, a Canadian young for his rank but innovative and resolute. His II Canadian Corps was not powerful enough to undertake TOTALIZE alone so he was given the use of the 51st Highland Division and British 33rd Armoured Brigade for Phase One and the 1st Polish Armoured Division for Phase Two. Even as the Poles were arriving from Bayeux to take up formation around Cormelles le Royal, the Phase One troops were setting out from Cormelles to assault the ridge, by night, across country and led by massive formations of tanks.

At this point it is relevant to point out two factors to the Poles' disadvantage. Firstly, elements of the division were still coming ashore to join an unknown corps only three days before the operation commenced, very little time for settling in and briefing, let alone specialised training for a role. Secondly the division's chief of staff, Colonel Jerzy Levittoux who was visiting Normandy to study the situation and brief his commander and staff, was unfortunately killed on 18 July, so that essential briefing was delayed. However on 7 August those considerations had no impact on the Polish rank and file as they prepared for their long awaited day of opportunity.

In front of the Poles, as also the Canadians and British, still awaited formidable German soldiers, among the best trained and highly motivated in the German army of *12.-SS Panzerdivision Hitlerjugend* (Hitler Youth), together with a full strength, fresh infantry division, 89.*Infanteriedivision Hufeisen* ("Horseshoe" after its divisional insignia), recently arrived from Norway. Even beyond the crest of the ridge the countryside would be undulating farmland presenting continuing opportunities for the defenders to hide and dig in their guns and mortars. Success of Simonds' unique tactics for Phase One would not in any way minimise the difficulties of Phase Two. In fact the precision of initial advance, which was possible – tanks in ranks of four equally spaced – around midnight of 7 August, would disintegrate in the normal chaos of battle; and the following troops would be striving across devastated ground with elements of the original battle plan requiring urgent adaptation or postponement.

Phase One was, in some ways, a simple plan based on seven columns of tanks and infantry driving directly through the German defences, reaching objectives along the summit of the ridge, digging in, and then challenging the enemy to counter-attack, which was the Germans' routine reaction. Through this area of continuing contention Phase Two lead troops would have to pass and develop the advance towards the eventual target of Falaise. There, in a southerly advance, it might be possible to link up with the Americans who could be swinging northwards from far in the west to achieve an encirclement of the entire German Army in Normandy.

There were seven Phase One columns but it is sufficient briefly to follow the left hand column which the Poles would have to follow. Near Cormelles, 1st Northamptonshire Yeomanry formed its 60 tanks in ranks of four. Behind the first squadron and ranks of flail tanks came a company of 1st Black Watch in armoured carriers called Kangaroos, an instant invention by Simonds. More tanks and infantry followed in a column of nearly 200 vehicles. Because the intervening villages were impassable the column had to advance across country. A brief but violent artillery barrage and a raid by several hundred bombers of the RAF eased the column's way but added to the existing devastation of the terrain. Crashing through the German defence lines the column occupied the summit village of Saint Aignan-de-Cramesnil and formed a defensive ring, open on the left or east side but linking into other British and Canadian lodgements on the west where the main Caen to Falaise road formed a centre line.

The column had fully occupied the vital village by early morning. It was midday by the time the German commander was able to launch a powerful riposte with tanks and infantry of the *Hitlerjugend*. The Yeomanry and Black Watch fought off the attack but it was into this cauldron of fire and smoke that the first Polish tanks had to pass a few yards away from the Northamptonshire crews. At this point it is relevant to give considerable detail about the first point of contact between Poles and Germans in Normandy. Some commentators have been unduly critical of the Poles (and II Canadian Corps, of which 1st Polish Armoured Division formed a part). Indeed the first impact caused many casualties and much frustration to the Polish tank men themselves. They must be absolved of any blame for any delay in what continued to be overall a unique and important breach of the German defences unparalleled in earlier Normandy battles around Caen.

At this point on 8 August the new arrivals were to be frustrated by one of several unforeseen circumstances favouring the enemy. Both the British Yeomanry, and the Canadian Sherbrooke Fusiliers on the other side of the main road, had found themselves at breakfast time solidly placed along the top of the ridge and with apparently undefended open country ahead. Both regiments were still near full strength. Officers of both units sought permission to keep going. This was denied, mainly because a USAAF raid was scheduled to hit the next line of German defences. In the convoluted system of communications between Allied units of varying arms, affected also by political considerations, it was not possible in the time available to cancel the USAAF raid which would have rained bombs down on the tank units if they had been further advanced. Because of bad aiming, bombs did indeed rain down on Allied units and the Poles themselves suffered severe casualties in areas that should have been safe from 'friendly fire'.

The delay meant that the empty country beyond the ridge summit was uncontested for seven hours during which the Germans were able to bring up substantial reinforcements. So the Poles had to attack head on into the one situation which TOTALIZE was intended to avoid, mass attack in daylight across open ground against enemy well-hidden and equipped with more powerful guns.

Furthermore, although the Yeomanry at troop and squadron level were just now, moment by moment, locating the new German gun positions they had no way of communicating this knowledge to Polish troop and squadron leaders. Not only was there a language problem but the two regiments involved were using different code words for their report lines and objectives (The Poles using names of Polish cities while the Yeomanry had been issued with names of Hollywood film stars). There is a tragic story of Lieutenant Tony Faulkner of the Yeomanry (whose tank had just been knocked out) frantically waving his beret at the first Polish tanks to try to warn them of their danger; whereat the Poles, assuming this to be a comradely act of welcome, waved their berets back.

A minor point of interest is that the Poles were instantly recognisable by their berets. They wore the normal British battle-dress. However the Polish habit was to pull the beret straight back and wear the badge, as well as badges of rank, central to the forehead. The British routinely pulled their berets over to the right with the badge only fixed over the left eye.

Sadly, even as the two Allies recognised each other, Polish tanks began to burn. The Yeomanry had advanced with an open left flank covered by woods burning from the RAF attack. Now, beyond those woods towards Conteville there was room for two armoured regiments to squeeze through. The Polish 2nd Armoured Regiment passed within yards of Lieutenant Faulkner's troop, fanning out past the chateau of Saint Aignan. Beyond and downhill the 24th *Uhlans* moved with an open left flank but needing to avoid further downhill motion for the enemy forces were now arriving on the next ridge towards Saint Sylvain. This was a lesser summit than Saint Aignan but still a formidable barrier with its wooded enclaves for German anti-tank guns.

The 2nd Armoured Regiment now suffered from another unforeseen occurrence. The Northamptonshire Yeomanry were contesting a very narrow but exceptionally deep ravine which, from aerial photos appeared to be merely a normal country track. It was wide enough for tanks to move through and deep enough for them to remain invisible to all around; this was well known to the Germans whose Corps Headquarters had been located nearby. *Panzers* down in the ravine therefore had a narrow tunnel view towards where the 2nd Armoured must pass across open ground at short range. The enthusiastic Polish advance became a duck shoot, the foremost Polish commanders had no idea where the shots were emanating from, the ravine and woods hiding the minimal flash and smoke of the enemy pieces.

Meanwhile the *Uhlans* were confronted by an even wider space leading to the woods around Saint Sylvain into which the German commander had interposed his reconnaissance regiment. Less motivated units than the two Polish regiments might have held off sooner. In the end more than forty Polish tanks were lost (in all some eighty tanks were destroyed, including British and German, within the view from the central point near Tony Faulkner's tank).

In terms of Normandy battles the Poles' loss was not catastrophic. The 2nd Northamptonshire Yeomanry had lost an equal number of tanks during GOODWOOD but within 36 hours were up to full strength again. There was an endless conveyor belt of new tanks available. A knocked out crew might only have to walk back a mile to RHQ to secure a new tank. However, whilst the reserve pool of British tank crews was adequate, the loss of one Polish soldier was much more significant in terms of finding replacements of appropriate skill. By evening of 8 of August 1st Armoured had at least pushed beyond the fatal ravine and consolidated on the next minor ridge around Robertmesnil.

Historians have focussed on that Polish first hour of drama and loss advancing from Saint Aignan. But what followed revealed the Poles beginning to demonstrate their power and resolution in a rarely mentioned action. On the evening of 8 August Major General Maczek had ordered his 3rd Rifle Brigade to pass through the tanks and deal with the Germans hidden in the woods around Robertmesnil. Although the Germans had begun to withdraw the Polish infantry pushed ahead in the dark and collected their first 48 prisoners of war. On the left flank Saint Sylvain was captured and in these operations much of the enemy's light armoured and reconnaissance force had been destroyed. At this point of crisis for the entire German army in Normandy the loss of one German soldier was much more critical than the loss of an Allied soldier. In respect of material, as the enemy were in constant retreat there was little opportunity for them to recover damaged vehicles or equipment whereas the Allies could carry out recovery at leisure.

Overnight on 8 August there occurred the next extraordinary event which dislocated all battle plans for the following day. Simonds had ordered another night march; after the success of the complex plan for seven columns to break through on the 7 August, he might well have expected a similar but lesser operation to achieve success on the next day. This would have left the Poles free to push forward on the 9 August. Human frailty intervened.

A Canadian 'Worthington Force' was formed consisting of a regiment of tanks and most of a battalion of infantry. This was despatched sideways of the main Caen to Falaise road in order to push around the hastily posted German defences, swing back and seize another dominating landmark. The column lost its way in the dark, veered to the left, laagered on an isolated slope, and at dawn found itself cut off by some distance from other Allied forward troops. It was then methodically eliminated by German armour. As the site lay away from the compass direction of the intended objective there was, for a time, complete ignorance and confusion at division and corps headquarters as to the whereabouts and development of this tragic last stand. Among search and rescue attempts the nearest Poles had to be diverted to try to locate Worthington Force, thus inevitably throwing previous plans out of gear and off course.

In spite of serious losses the German defenders were still in considerable force and had brought in another fresh infantry division. On 9 August 24th *Uhlans* reported seeing 10-15 tanks of 'Tiger type'. These may have been Panthers or self-propelled guns of a model which the Poles had never encountered before. But they pressed forward in the direction of Soignolles, reaching the commune of La Croix already some two mile beyond their Saint Aignan start line. At this point they became exposed to anti-tank fire at long, but effective range from the thick woodland around Quesnay which the Canadians had not yet been able to clear.

It was 1st Armoured Regiment which had been diverted to the west and ordered to try to contact the beleaguered Worthington Force. They soon perceived the smoke of what was already a fight to the death by the trapped Canadians. However, in an effort to relieve the Canadians they had again to cross open ground. An experienced *SS Panzer* battle group had completely surrounded Worthington Force and could defend its own rear with the deadly 88m guns. The 1st Armoured were exposed and committed to a fierce battle with resultant casualties. In the end, as Worthington Force was completely destroyed, the Poles reported only seven Canadian survivors being found. In due course some fifty other Canadians filtered through to 1st Armoured. The regiment's day had been taken up by this diversion, also distorting the division's lines of advance which should have been more directly to the south and south east.

On 10 August having cleared Soignolles the Poles felt the full blast of routine German counterattacks there but were able after fierce fighting to repel the enemy. The loss of impetus related to the massacre of Worthington Force and the problems of clearing Quesnay Wood persuaded Simonds to halt TOTALIZE in order to reform and plan for another disciplined attack.

Major General Maczek later commented that the width of front allowed to II Canadian Corps by Montgomery was not sufficient to allow adequate armoured manoeuvre. This was evidenced, among other ways, by the problems in working around the guns in Quesnay Woods which were effective at 2,000 yards. Despite the convulsions of their first hour at Saint Aignan, and the confusion of later events, the 1st Polish Armoured Division had won ground to a point as much as 4 miles beyond

Saint Aignan chateau. The entire TOTALIZE advance had driven 9 miles through the German lines in three days This contrasted with the first 40 days after D-Day when an advance of 500 yards was considered fair reward for high casualties.

Although the attackers were faced by only a relatively thin crust of German defenders those defenders included some of the best troops, armed with the best weapons, and evincing the highest morale that the German army could provide. Some commentators have blamed the soldiers in the field for the fact that TOTALIZE Phase Two developed slowly when related to Montgomery's ambitious intentions and inflated declarations. The French historian, Ludovic Florin places the blame much higher in the planning and command structure. He assesses that any tardiness was due more to attitudes at the highest command level producing 'density of the hierarchy, lack of flexibility and [reluctance to permit] individual initiative'.

To cap all the confusion of war, on 11 August Montgomery instructed Crerar, Simonds's superior, that the central plan of action had now been changed. The TOTALIZE force in its new mission would not be aiming south east to halt and encircle the Germans on the banks of the Seine in the long intended wide encirclement plan. They would now be directed straight south to Falaise, attempting an encirclement there by linking up with the Americans advancing from the south. In fact this would eventually occur in the countryside around Mont Ormel, a shorter encirclement. With this in mind Simonds began to plan Operation TRACTABLE.

Urgency was imperative. It was decided to use much of the TOTALIZE system, attacking after a brief mass aerial and artillery bombardment, advancing in formations of massed tanks closely supported by carrier infantry, but this time in daylight, using smoke to confuse the enemy. The Polish and Canadian armoured divisions would lead off from around Soignolles towards Falaise. Once the way had been opened, 1st Polish Armoured Division would swing away eastwards towards Ermes (in the general direction of Mount Ormel but not, as yet, with that final destination). This would give the Poles greater opportunity for manoeuvre than in TOTALIZE. The attack would be launched on 14 August with a raid by 800 RAF bombers.

Again fate conspired to disrupt what appeared to be a feasible, fairly straightforward advance. Three unfortunate Allied errors contributed to a near disaster. The first occurred on the night of 13 August. A Canadian staff officer accidentally drove into the Germans lines and was killed. On his body were found complete plans of the TRACTABLE attack. The Germans immediately concentrated all their most powerful remaining forces directly in front of the planned attack.

The second catastrophe occurred when the RAF raid commenced. Canadian tanks crews reacted in the fashion of all Allied tank crews since D-Day. They sent up yellow smoke to mark their positions and prevent 'friendly fire'. At the commencement of TOTALIZE the master bombers had successfully used red and green flares to mark their targets. Now, for some reason, it was decided to mark the bombers' targets with yellow smoke. Someone, or some many, at the highest level of inter Allied command should have been aware of this unfortunate coincidence. In the event some of the bomb aimers logically aimed at the yellow smoke and thus at their own friends. The error cost over 400 Polish and Canadian casualties, with 165 killed, as well as massive disruption at tank troop and squadron levels. Whereas the erratic bombing at the beginning of TOTALIZE fell mainly in rear echelon areas and did not immediately affect lead troops, the TRACTABLE error affected the spearhead armour and had the impact almost of an enemy counterattack.

The sufferings of the Poles under two 'friendly fire' attacks from the air in their first week of action deserve a further explanation. Perhaps the clearest summary of the facts are contained in the report by Air Chief Marshal Sir Arthur Harris, Commander-in-Chief, Bomber Command, written on 15 August 1944. He reported that during the TRACTABLE raid 811 planes unloaded 553 tons of bombs on seven targets and three planes were lost. As to the incident at Saint Aignan-de-Cramesnil 14 planes were found to have bombed in error. A total of 77 planes were judged culpable over the period. Harris had, it is true, pointed out the risks in this type of operation but the army had accepted responsibility and insisted on continuing. He pointed out that Bomber Command air crew were trained so that each aeroplane navigated its own course and bombed its target as an individual unit, normally at night and responding to flares marking the general target area. They were not used to mass formation attack in daylight.

However, Harris complained that the army had not advised his Command that the tanks would be using yellow smoke as their defensive signal. Yet he himself quoted Canadian Army Operations Standing Orders, Paragraph 8, stating that yellow or orange smoke or flares should be used by ground troops as a signal to friendly aircraft. So did nobody at the highest level when planning TRACTABLE ask the obvious question about identification? Did nobody in RAF liaison notice that yellow smoke had been used by tank crews over the 68 days since D-Day?

A third error was at a lower level of military intelligence. On the map the River Laison appeared to be an inoffensive minor stream, easily traversed by tanks. In fact in the attack area it was of precisely the dimensions to form a natural tank trap: the exact width into which an advancing tank would fit and sufficient depth to ensure that when the tank dropped on to the river bed it was too deep to climb out. First attacks shuddered and halted while Bailey bridges were brought up and erected under fire.

The Polish tank crews therefore spent much of the 14th waiting for space to open up as the Canadians overcame their initial difficulties. Polish Rifles cleared Quesnay Wood which had been such a thorn in the division's side previously. They also occupied the town of Potigny. It was on 15 August that 1st Polish Armoured Division launched into what has been described by Canadian historian R.J. Jarymowycz as 'a textbook example of an armoured division in action'. In more picturesque terms

Florin wrote that 'the Poles entered into the dance with a renewed fervour for 15 August is the day of the Feast of the Soldier in Poland'. Led by 10th Dragoons they drove forward to the banks of the River Dives and crossed this by morning.

On 16 August Maczek formed three battle groups, each of one tank regiment and one infantry battalion, probing around the flank of *12.-SS Panzerdivision Hitlerjugend* until space was found to the south east. This enabled the division to push on to the vicinity of the strategic town of Trun, well south of Falaise. Meanwhile in Falaise itself *12.-SS Panzerdivision Hitlerjugend* still resisted, if in greatly reduced numbers. The official TRACTABLE plan ('take Falaise!') ended on that day but for the Poles it was simply a continuing sweep around the German flank without necessarily having an 'Operation' format attached to it.

In view of contemporary complaints, and more recent historians' criticisms of slow progress during the advances of 8-19 August, it is relevant to compare that progress with the period 6 June to 6 August. As already cited, for most of that time an advance of 500 yards was considered laudable, if indeed any advance were made at all. Even Operation GOODWOOD, at very high price, had only effectively moved a couple of miles forward of the River Orne. Now here was 1st Polish Armoured Division advancing from Saint Aignan-de-Cramesnil to Hill 262, a distance of 30 miles as the crow flies, and many more miles in side attacks and diversions. For TOTALIZE a total was recorded of 429 Prisoners of War yielding to the Poles; and for TRACTABLE 5,113, in addition to substantial German casualties and losses of material.

Whilst many other Allied units contributed to closing the so-called 'Falaise trap', it was the Polish armoured hammer which slammed the door in the face of a hundred thousand trapped enemy troops.

Normandy, August 1944

78. Embarkation, London, July 1944. The 1st Polish Armoured Division prepares to cross the English Channel to France. Elements of the Division sailed from the ports of London, Dover and Southampton at the end of July. The troops are carrying their personal equipment. The vessels lined up alongside the dock by the cranes are "Liberty Ships" built in US dockyards to a standard design to meet the massive demand for wartime shipping and to replace the heavy losses suffered by the Allied merchant fleets due to U-boat and other attacks at sea. Several such ships would be required to move an armoured division across the English Channel. (PISM)

79. Crossing the Channel, the Thames Estuary, late July 1944. One of the transports carrying soldiers of the 1st Polish Armoured Division heads out of the Thames towards Normandy. The soldiers are all wearing life-jackets, a sensible precaution in case of sudden emergency. The main threat to cross-channel shipping at this time of the war was the mine. An escorting Royal Navy corvette is in the distance. On the horizon can be seen the towers of one of the Maunsell "Sea Forts", these structures were mounted on the sea bed and were intended to supplement the anti-aircraft defences of the Port of London. The Forts consisted of seven inter-connected towers, four of which mounted 3.7 heavy anti-aircraft guns. (PISM)

80. Unloading vehicles, Mulberry Harbour "B", Arromanches, Normandy July/August 1944. HMS LCT 1136, a Royal Navy LCT (Landing Craft Tank) Mk IV, heads for the shore carrying a full load of jeeps (in the foreground) and lorries. In the background a Liberty Ship continues unloading. (PISM)

81. Unloading vehicles, Mulberry Harbour "B", Arromanches, Normandy July/August 1944. A M5 Armoured ambulance is loaded into a LCT alongside a Liberty Ship. The vehicle is assigned to the 2nd Armoured Regiment and carries its Arm of Service number "52". A Red Cross marking can be seen on the right side of the vehicle. A Bedford QL truck has already been loaded into the LCT. (PISM)

82. Unloading vehicles, Mulberry Harbour "B", Arromanches, Normandy July 1944. By this time the British Mulberry was the only one in operation. The US Mulberry Harbour "A" at Omaha Beach having being destroyed during the great storm of 19 June 1944. HMS LCT 1103, a LCT Mk IV, has moved up to one of the pontoon causeways linking the harbour to the shore and vehicles are being guided down its lowered ramp. The leading vehicle is a Bedford QL truck. One of the standard wartime trucks of the British Army it could carry 11 passengers or a load of 3 tons. It was produced in a variety of models to serve a wide range of roles. The chalk markings under the windscreen probably relate to loading-unloading procedures. A circled White-Star Allied recognition marking is carried on the vehicle's cab roof. Awaiting its turn to unload is a 3 ton GS Ford O1T V8 truck. Above the LCT can be seen a barrage balloon intended to deter attacks by dive-bombers and low-flying aircraft. (PISM)

83. Divisional Orders Group, Normandy, August 1944. Major General Stanisław Mazcek conducts an "O" (Orders) Group planning meeting with his staff officers. General Maczek was one of the leading Allied commanders of armour in the North-Western European Campaign of 1944-45 with a long and extensive military experience from the Polish-Soviet war to the 1940 campaign in France. To assist him in his command tasks he had assembled a small but very capable group of officers to command the formations and units in his division, many of whom had served with him in various appointments in the pre-War Polish Army and then during the Polish and French campaigns. Many of the division's officers had also, since their arrival in England, attended a wide variety of courses which helped develop their technical and professional expertise. General Maczek's trust in the professionalism of his officers and the training of his soldiers would be both demonstrated and rewarded during the forthcoming operations TOTALIZE and TRACTABLE. (PISM)

84. General Montgomery Visit, Normandy, 5 August 1944. General Montgomery, in characteristic casual style, shares a joke with Major General Mazcek during an afternoon long visit to the 1st Polish Armoured Division. As was his practice during such visits, Montgomery fully briefed the division's senior commanders on his plans so that all would be aware of his intentions. This visit also resulted in a more favourable impression of the 21st Army Group Commander than was the case during his previous visit on 13 April 1944 (see photo 73). The 1st Polish together with the 4th Canadian Armoured (which deployed to Normandy at the same time) were the last armoured divisions to reinforce Montgomery's 21st Army Group until 1945. (PISM)

85. Second Armoured Regiment, Mail Distribution, Normandy 3 Aug 1944. Staff Sergeant A.L. Jarzembowski distributes mail to members of the 2nd Armoured Regiment who will probably be then be responsible for further onward distribution. Prompt delivery of personal mail was regarded as a vital component of maintaining morale, and great efforts were made by the Army Postal authorities to ensure that regular deliveries were made to the troops in the field. (AHA)

86. Bofors Anti-Aircraft Gun, **Normandy, August 1944**. The crew of a heavily camouflaged Bofors 40mm anti-aircraft gun scan the sky for enemy aircraft. Each armoured regiment and each armoured reconnaissance regiment in a British type armoured division had an anti-aircraft platoon of six Crusader II/III anti-aircraft tanks. Providing anti-aircraft protection for other elements of the division was the duty of the 1st Anti-Aircraft Regiment, the divisional light anti-aircraft regiment with a total of 54 × 40mm Bofors guns mounted on Morris C9/B lorries. The gun usually had a crew of four. Only two of which can be see here. The detachment commander, with the binoculars, would designate the target. The loader, holding the clip of 40mm rounds would be expected to maintain the flow of ammunition to sustain the gun's rate of fire of 120 rounds per minute. It was this Polish unit that suffered 44 killed and wounded during the miss-aimed American bombing on 8 August. (PISM)

87. Crusader III Anti-Aircraft tank, **Normandy, August 1944**. A Crusader III anti-aircraft tank MK II, 2nd Armoured Regiment, with its crew. With the significantly reduced threat from the Luftwaffe, the Crusader with its 2 × 20mm Oerlikon cannon, was often used against ground targets. It was particular effective in this role during the fighting on the *Maczuga* 19-21 August 1944. Note the crewman, extreme left, has borrowed an American M3 "Grease-gun" (so nicknamed because of its resemblance to a mechanic's greaser tool) substituting the standard issue Mk III Sten –gun seen here, without a magazine fitted, held by the crewman, third from left. (AHA)

88. Forward Headquarters, Normandy, August 1944. Headquarters of 1st Polish Armoured Division. Note the divisional insignia on two of the signs. Directional arrows direct visitors, such as dispatch riders to a particular ACV (Armoured Command Vehicle). These would be camouflaged AEC Dorchester ACV vehicles and office trucks used by senior commanders and their staffs. The sign in Polish in the centre directs visitors to use existing tracks, as a profusion of vehicle tyre-marks would show up on aerial photographs and allow enemy photo-graphic interpreters to identify the location as a potential high-value target for either artillery strikes (if in range) or bombing raids. (PISM)

89. Casualty Collection Point, Normandy, August 1944. A Polish Medical Unit, a Casualty Collection Point prepares for action. An Austin "Katie" ambulance is on the right, so nicknamed because of its British Army K2 designation, the standard British Army ambulance. The three ton vehicle could accommodate ten casualties or four stretcher cases. There is no indication that the facility is currently operational and is therefore probably still being set up. The 3 ton GS Ford O1T V8 truck on the left has been backed into a tent, perhaps to provider shelter for treatment of casualties. Stores have been unloaded near the front of the truck. The figure second from the left could be a padre. The divisional medical services consisted of the *10 Lekka Kompania Sanitarnia* (10 Light Medical Company); *11 Kompania Sanitarnia* (11 Medical Company); *1 Polowa Stacja Opatrunkowa* (1 Field Operating Station) and the *1 Polowa Higieny Polowie* (1 Field Hygiene Section). (PISM)

90. Caen, Normandy, July 1944. A War Memorial to the French dead of the First World War stands in the *Place Foch* in the centre of the shattered city of Caen, surrounded by destroyed and damaged buildings. Caen had been a key objective for the British 2nd Army after landing on D-Day. The Germans also saw its possession as of vital importance to their defence of Normandy and concentrated most of their available *Panzer* forces in its defence. As a result a series of bitter and costly battles raged around the city during June and early July, until most of the city finally fell on 9 July after an assault supported by heavy bombing which devastated the city. The Poles arrived in Normandy some weeks after the city had been completely evacuated by the Germans. By then the roads had been cleared of rubble to allow for the passage of military traffic. (PISM)

91. Normandy, August 1944. This soldier is wearing a Dispatch Riders Helmet and appears to have a Red Cross armband on his left arm. He stands in front of a 24th Lancers Stuart Mk V light tank. He well may be a medical orderly attached to the reconnaissance platoon. (PISM)

92. Polish Officer, Normandy, August 1944. A Polish infantry officer stands in front of the same Stuart Mk V light tank. He is wearing battledress. Goggles and binoculars are slung round his neck. He wears his pistol holster hung from his belt on his left hip. The Stuart behind him is one of the 11 vehicles from the 24th *Uhlans* Reconnaissance platoon and carries its Arm of Service number of "53" on its right track guard. Above it is the Winged Hussar divisional insignia. On the left track guard is the nationality marking "PL". The officer may well be from a company from the 10th Dragoons, the motor battalion supporting the 10th Armoured Cavalry Brigade, detached to provide infantry support to the 24th Lancers. A reconnaissance platoon of light tanks was attached to each armoured regiment. Supplied under lend-lease by the United States this 15 ton tank had a speed of 40 mph. It was fitted with a 37mm gun. First entering service with the British 8th Army in 1941 its reliability and effectiveness in the medium tank role earned it the nickname of "Honey". By 1944 it was totally obsolete. Many units actually removed the turret, substituting a 0.50 calibre machine gun on a ring mounting, believing that the 360 degree visibility this modification afforded was a more effective means of protection than the ineffective armament. After the Normandy Campaign the 10th Mounted Rifles Assault Platoon similarly modified its Stuart tanks designating them "Ducks". (PISM)

93. Holy Communion, Normandy, August, 1944. A Polish Chaplain conducts a Communion service for tank crews. The bonnet of a jeep has been turned into a temporary altar. In action, chaplains were encouraged to be as far forward as possible, both to assist in medical support and to provide spiritual comfort to the wounded. In many armoured regiments across 21st Army Group chaplains often took on the difficult task of extracting the remains of crewmen from their knocked-out vehicles for burial. The tank on the left is a Firefly, the other a standard Sherman V. (PISM)

94. Pre-Battle Preparation, Normandy, August 1944. A Polish tank crew prepare a bivouac, digging a trench behind their vehicle that will be reversed over it, affording some protection from shelling and bombing (see photo 108). Note that this particular tank has had its side hull Allied recognition star obscured, to prevent it's use as at targeting point for enemy gunners. The turret 0.50 calibre heavy machine gun has been dismounted, probably for cleaning. In the centre of the photo is a 17 pounder equipped Firefly. Although much of the barrel is obscured, the distinctive turret extension, designed to accommodate the gun's powerful recoil, and with its attached radio compartment, can be seen. (PISM)

95. Sherman and Crusader Anti-Aircraft Tanks, Normandy, August 1944. A group of at least three Sherman tanks and two Crusader anti-aircraft tanks. The tanks may be from the headquarters of an unidentified armoured regiment with the anti-aircraft tanks providing security against air attacks. Attached to each Armoured Regiment Headquarters troop was a platoon of six Crusader anti-aircraft tanks. Although the Allies enjoyed almost total air superiority over Normandy, German aircraft were able to make the occasional attack, as on the morning of 16 August when Focke-Wulf 190 fighter-bombers attacked the Jort bridgehead inflicting casualties in a rare daylight sortie by the Luftwaffe. (PISM)

96. Stuarts and Cromwell tanks, Normandy, August 1944. Stuart V (foreground tank named 'Janka') and Cromwell tanks from the 10th Mounted Rifles move along a road somewhere in Normandy. The 10th Mounted Rifles was the 1st Polish Armoured Division's Armoured Renaissance Regiment and was equipped with Cromwell cruiser tanks. Unlike the armoured regiments which contained a number of Firefly tanks with 17 pounder guns the Armoured Reconnaissance Regiment had no such support. Until the supply of the Challenger, a vehicle based on a lengthened Cromwell hull and capable of mounting a 17 pounder (which did not enter service until after the end of the Normandy Campaign) troops of Achilles self-propelled guns were detached from the 1st Anti-Tank Regiment to provide 17 pounder support.

97. Shermans and Fireflys, Normandy, August 1944. Polish tank crews from an unidentified Armoured Regiment make final checks before moving forward. Most of the tanks are Sherman Mk V, however the two in the centre foreground are Fireflys mounting 17 pounder guns with the gun barrels secured over the engine compartment to avoid damage when moving forward in closely formed columns, such as at night. Both Fireflys mount 0.50 machine guns on their turrets. On two tanks the white-star recognition marking is visible while the other tanks in the formation have obscured theirs to avoid providing an aiming mark for enemy tank and anti-tank gunners. (PISM)

98. Ken Tout, August 1944. Aged 18, Ken Tout was conscripted into "C" Squadron, 1st Northamptonshire Yeomanry as a Sherman tank gunner. His first experience of war was on 30 June 1944, in Normandy when he fired his first shot. His regiment fought in the opening stages of TOTALIZE, and he witnessed the 1st Polish Armoured Division advance into their first combat on 8 August 1944. In Holland, in October 1944, he suffered very serious injuries when his Sherman tank rolled off the road into a canal, seeing no more service for the rest of the war. Post-war he was ordained and worked closely with a number of charitable organisations. In 1985 he wrote his first book *Tank! 40 Hours of Battle, August 1944* an account of his wartime experiences which has since become a classic personal account of armoured warfare in North-West Europe in 1944. Since then he has written further books and articles, given talks and interviews and has provided, for many historians, including the authors of this book, his eye-witness insights into one of the most dramatic periods in the history of armoured warfare. (Ken Tout)

99. Lieutenant General Guy Simonds, Normandy, August 1944. Lieutenant General Guy Simonds (1903-74), GOC II Canadian Corps conferring with one of his officers. A Major in 1938 he was a Major General by 1943. He commanded Canadian divisions in Sicily and Italy and took over command of II Canadian Corps in January 1944. Responsible for the innovative plan of Operation TOTALIZE in August 1944. He was highly thought of by General Montgomery and later took over command of 1st Canadian Army during the absence of its commander General "Harry" Crerar due to illness. Post war he became Chief of the General Staff of the Canadian Army in 1951. Moving around the battlefield Lieutenant General Simonds used a converted Staghound armoured car as his command vehicle, with the turret removed, which allowed more room for additional radios and staff. The T17E1 Staghound was an American designed heavy armoured vehicle which saw service with British, Polish and Commonwealth forces in the later part of the war. (PISM)

100. Preparing to Advance, Normandy, 8 August 1944. Elements of the 1st Polish Armoured Division wait to advance on Falaise, together with 4th Canadian Armoured Division, as part of Operation TOTALIZE Phase 2. Earlier that morning Canadian and British infantry from II Canadian Corps had broken through the German lines during their surprise night-time advance. These troops and vehicles are waiting for the preparatory US 8th Air Force bombing of the forward German positions to begin. On the left a column of troop-carrying Bedford QL trucks and on the right a column of M5 half-tracks led by a Morris Light Reconnaissance car. This lightly armoured (3.7 ton) vehicle could mount a Bren gun or Boys Anti-tank rifle. Here it is probably serving as an escort vehicle for the truck columns formed up behind.
(PISM)

101. Normandy, 8 August 1944. Elements of the 1st Polish Armoured Division wait to move off as part of Phase 2 of Operation TOTALIZE as bombs begin to explode to their rear. During the preparatory bombing, two groups of attacking USAAF bombers veered off course and dropped their bombs on the outskirts of Caen, causing serious damage and casualties. Most were suffered by Canadian units but the 1st Light Anti-Aircraft Regiment of the 1st Polish Armoured Division suffered 44 killed and wounded. Also the Canadian 4th and 7th medium artillery regiments, which were supposed to provide artillery support, lost many of their 5.5 artillery pieces. So surprised were some of the victims of the bombing that they believed that the attacking planes were captured aircraft flown by *Luftwaffe* crews! This photo shows the same vehicle column as in the previous image but from a different angle as the Polish soldiers watch the start of the miss-directed bombing attack to their rear. (PISM)

102. Normandy, 8 August 1944. Smoke continues to rise from the outskirts of Caen following the American bombing. These jeeps belonging to 1st Polish Armoured Division are covered by camouflage nets. In the background a motorcycle dispatch rider can be seen. The main bombing attack proved to be disappointing as only two German artillery batteries were assessed as having been destroyed as a result. (PISM)

103. Shermans, Normandy, 8 August, 1944. Despite the misdirected USAAF bombing, the 1st Polish Armoured Division, led by 2nd Armoured Regiment supported by the 24th Uhlans, crossed its TOTALIZE Phase 2 start-line precisely on time at 13.55 hours, and immediately met with stiff resistance suffering serious losses, forcing both regiments to withdrew and regroup. By the end of the day 10th Armoured Cavalry Brigade had lost 57 tanks including 24 classified "Z" requiring "extensive repair or replacement". One of the casualties was Captain Marian Piwonski commander of the 1st Squadron, 24th *Uhlans* killed by artillery fire. General Maczek blamed difficult terrain which greatly favoured the German defenders, and the restricted deployment area laid down by the operation's planners. The tank on the right may belong to a platoon or squadron commander directing those under his command forward. It is well protected with spare track-links fitted to its front as added protection against German tank and anti-tank guns. Note that the Sherman on the left has it's right track fitted in reverse to normal practice? (PISM)

104. Convoy on the move, Normandy, August 1944. A convoy of lorries, at least one of which is a Bedford QL, and jeeps makes its way forward past a Sherman tank through the dust clouds thrown up by the movement of so many vehicles (which often attracted enemy artillery fire), during the hot dry Normandy summer. Some of the lorries and jeeps are pulling trailers and motorcycle dispatch riders move alongside the column. (PISM)

105. Achilles and Cromwells, Jort, Normandy, 15 August 1944. The 10th Mounted Rifles Battlegroup (Major Jan Maciejowski commanding), advance to seize the bridges over the River Dives at Jort. The battlegroup is re-enforced with a number of Achilles, with their 17 pounder guns, from the 1st Anti-Tank Regiment. Here, mixed elements of the battlegroup move forward. On the left of the photo is the rear of a Cromwell and in the centre, camouflaged with foliage to break up its outline is an Achilles. On the right three more advance with another Cromwell to their rear. (PISM)

106. Cromwell burning, Normandy, August 1944. A knocked-out Cromwell tank burns. The vehicle is from the 10th Mounted Rifles the division's Armoured Reconnaissance Regiment. The 30-ton Cromwell was the first truly reliable British built Cruiser tank equipping all the Armoured Reconnaissance Regiments in 1st Polish, the British Guards and 11th Armoured Divisions, but not the Canadian Army. It also was operated by all the armoured regiments in the British 7th Armoured Division, "the Desert Rats". It was fast (35 mph) and maneuverable and felt to be particularly suited for the reconnaissance role. The Cromwell was comparable in amour protection to the Sherman and mounted a similar MV 75mm gun. Unlike the Sherman it could not be modified to take the 17 pounder. To meet this deficiency the Challenger, based on a larger version of the Cromwell hull, which could mount a 17 pounder was developed but entered service only after the end of the Normandy campaign. (PISM)

107. Cromwell overturned, Normandy, August 1944. Polish soldiers attempt to rescue the crew from the turret of an overturned Cromwell. The vehicle is also from the 10th Mounted Rifles. On its glacis plate is the triangle marking for the Regiment's "A" Squadron. Smoke is still rising from a nearby crater. Just visible in the background is the smoldering Cromwell seen in the previous photo 103.(PISM)

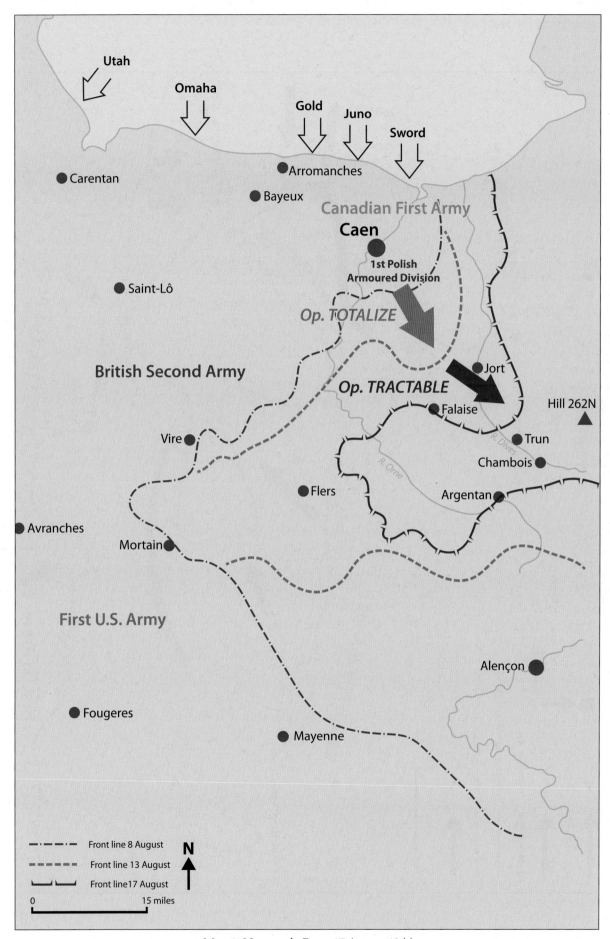

Map 1 Normandy Front 17 August 1944

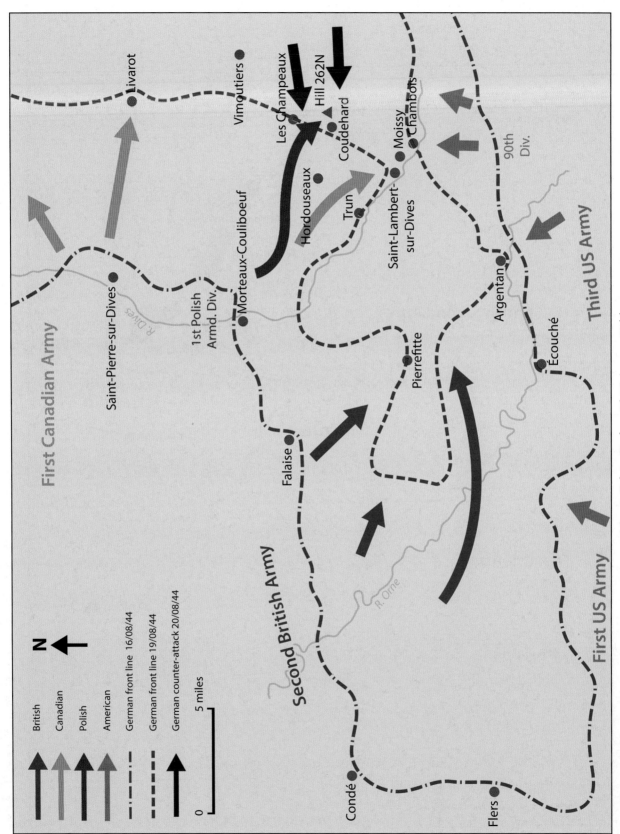

Map 2 Falaise Pocket 16-20 August 1944

First Canadian Army

Second British Army

First US Army

Third US Army

Livarot

Vimoutiers

Les Champeaux

Hill 262N

Coudehard

Moissy

Chambois

90th Div.

Hordouseaux

Trun

Saint-Lambert-sur-Dives

Morteaux-Couliboeuf

Saint-Pierre-sur-Dives

1st Polish Armd. Div.

R. Dives

Pierrefitte

Argentan

Écouché

Falaise

R. Orne

Condé

Flers

N

British
Canadian
Polish
American

German front line 16/08/44
German front line 19/08/44
German counter-attack 20/08/44

0   5 miles

ii

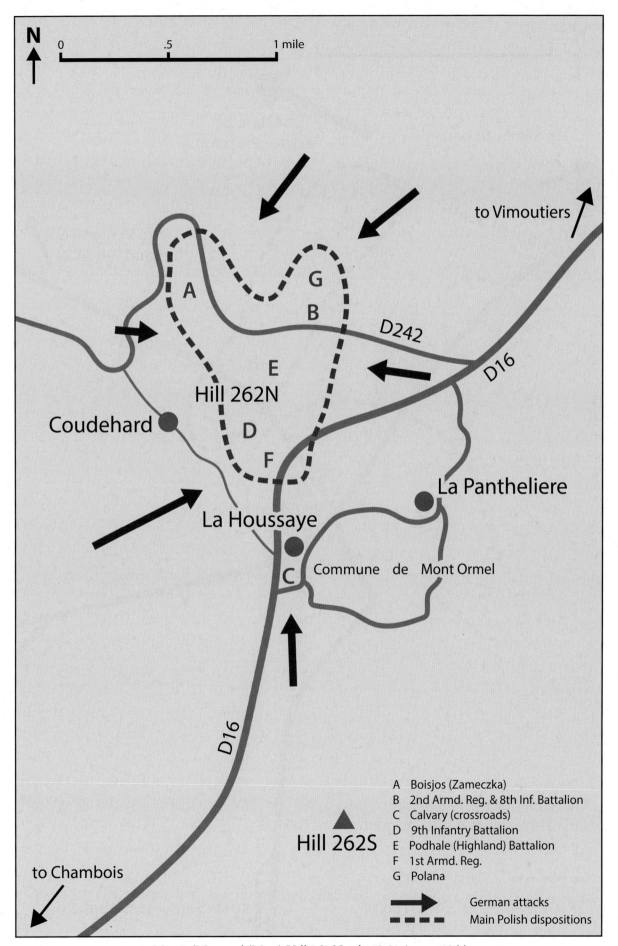

N

0   .5   1 mile

to Vimoutiers

A

G

B

D242

D16

E

Hill 262N

Coudehard

D

F

La Pantheliere

La Houssaye

Commune   de   Mont Ormel

C

D16

Hill 262S

to Chambois

A   Boisjos (Zameczka)
B   2nd Armd. Reg. & 8th Inf. Battalion
C   Calvary (crossroads)
D   9th Infantry Battalion
E   Podhale (Highland) Battalion
F   1st Armd. Reg.
G   Polana

➤   German attacks
▪▪▪   Main Polish dispositions

Map 3 'Maczuga' (Mace) Hill 262 North, 19-21 August 1944

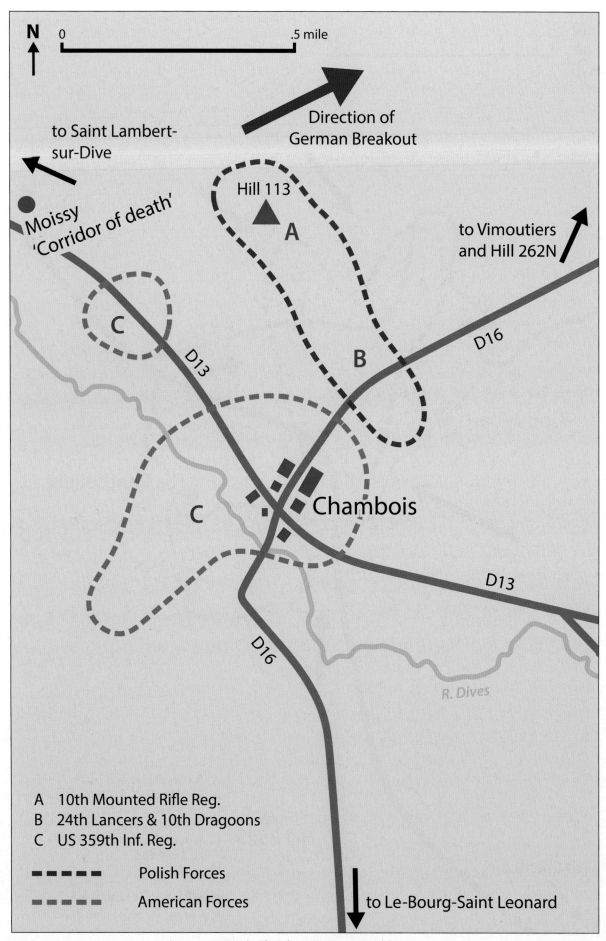

N

0 .5 mile

Direction of
German Breakout

to Saint Lambert-
sur-Dive

Moissy
'Corridor of death'

Hill 113

A

to Vimoutiers
and Hill 262N

C

D13

B

D16

C

Chambois

D13

D16

R. Dives

A 10th Mounted Rifle Reg.
B 24th Lancers & 10th Dragoons
C US 359th Inf. Reg.

Polish Forces

American Forces

to Le-Bourg-Saint Leonard

Map 4 Chambois 19 August 1944

A. Normandy, France, 1944. A Polish officer from the 2nd Armoured Regiment, 1st Polish Armoured Division, and a British Cromwell tank commander from the Royal Tank Corps shake hands on meeting on the fields of Normandy. (Reconstruction).

B. Normandy, France, 1944. A Polish tank commander rests on his Cromwell tank. The Cromwell was used by the 1st Polish Armoured Division's Armoured Reconnaissance Regiment, the *10 Pulk Strzelcow Konnych* (10th Mounted Rifle Regiment). (Reconstruction)

C. Normandy, France, 1944. A Polish tank commander checks his position, using a map from his British Army issue map case. He wears his beret in the Polish style, pulled to the rear, rather than the side which was the case in the British and Canadian armies. On his beret, centred, is the Polish Eagle national symbol below that his rank badge, the single star of a 2nd Lieutenant. His googles are essential in the dusty conditions of Normandy. (Reconstruction)

D. Normandy, France, 1944. The same tank as seen in photo F. (Reconstruction)

E. Normandy, France, 1944. A Polish tank commander pointing out 'in no uncertain terms' with his Webley pistol, captures a *Waffen-SS* soldier. Note the strap on the middle thigh is for the Mk 1 pistol holster, issued to tank crews, which was later modified and carried from the hip. (Reconstruction).

'The *Maczuga* (Mace) Hill 262N, Mont Ormel, 20 August 1944' by Peter Dennis.
The reconstructed scene depicts an eyewitness account by the commander of the 2nd Armoured Regiment, of a close-quarter action, typifying the engagements experienced by the besieged Polish units on the Mace (the attack was successfully repulsed without further loss) - "At the same time a second group of 2-3 company-strong Germans managed to encroach upon our woodlet, surprising the tank platoon that had secured the L ridge, and attacked us from the rear. Preoccupied with firing immediately in front of our field of vision

we became aware of our situation when the Germans started throwing grenades and several devil-may-care Germans started to actually mount our Shermans from 1st Squadron. This squadron started to independently withdraw their tanks. Some commanders started to fire backwards from their anti-aircraft machine guns, the tank gunners firing forward from their guns. When the anti-aircraft guns had run out of ammunition, the tank commanders actually pulled out their revolvers and tried to halt the tide of *Hitlerjugend* scrambling onto the tanks". Stanisław Koszutski *Wspomnienia z różnych pobojowisk*, London, 1972.

F. Normandy, France, 1944. A Polish tank commander, stands in front of a Sherman tank. He has discarded his battledress jacket a result of the Normandy summer. Round his neck hang a pair of binoculars. His map case hangs over his left shoulder and he wears his pistol (British issue Webley) holster on his right hip secured to his belt. Note: the tank is a Sherman M4A1 (British Army designation Sherman II) which was not used by Polish forces in Normandy. It is being used here, and in subsequent images solely for representational purposes. (Reconstruction).

G. Normandy, France, 1944. The tank commander , 2nd Lieutenant, has removed his battledress jacket and his Royal Armoured Corp Mk II helmet. Battledress (original) detail, left black shoulder strap, 10th Armoured Cavalry, commemorating the pre-war Brigade nicknamed 'The Black Devils'. Orange Lanyard, 2nd Armoured Regiment, Poland shoulder title, worn on both sleeves, divisional insignia the helmet of a Polish Winged Hussar.

Sherman V (M4A4)

Sherman VC Firefly

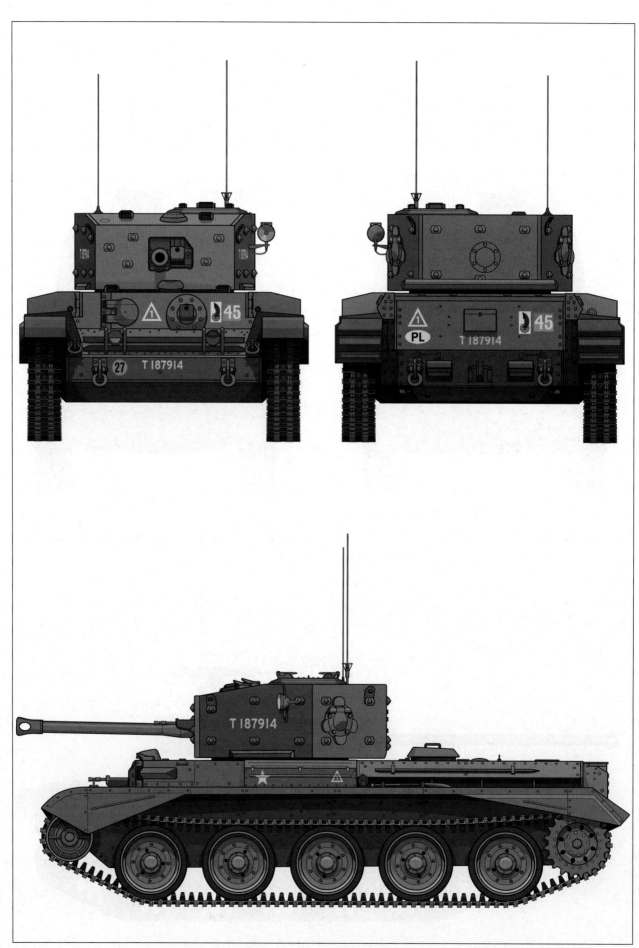

Cruiser VIII (A27) Cromwell VII

17 pounder, Self-Propelled, Achilles

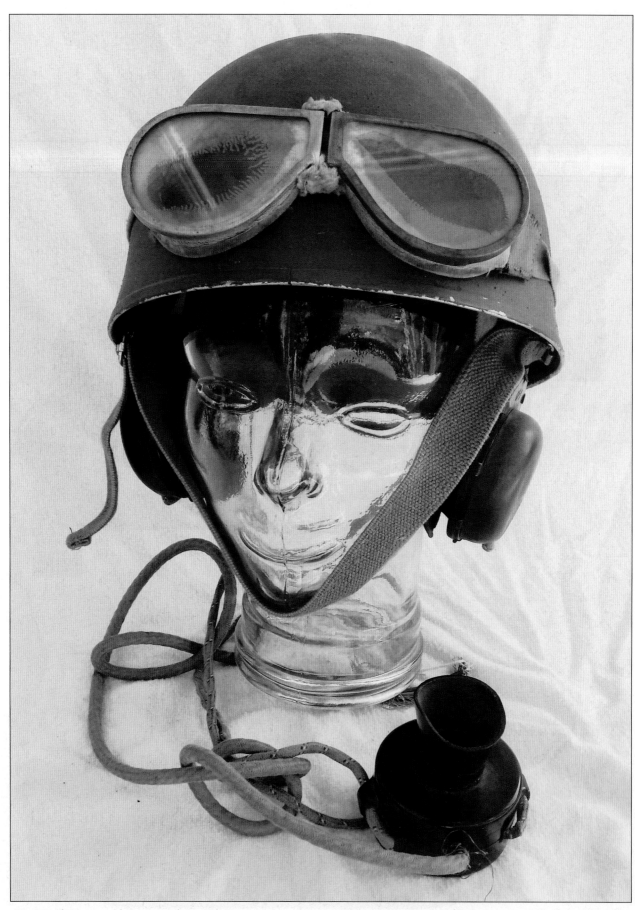

H. Royal Armoured Corps Helmet Mk II. Issued to armoured vehicle crews. It could be worn over vehicle headphones as seen here. Note the microphone. Being rimless the helmet was easier to wear and yet still be able to operate the equipment inside the cramped confines of a tank, which would be difficult wearing the standard infantry helmet.

108. Sherman Replacement, Normandy, August 1944. Polish soldiers prepare a shelter against possible shell-fire and bombing raids. The Sherman is a probably a replacement vehicle for a previous casualty. The Arm of Service number "473" over the left hand track shows it is from the Divisional Replacement Centre. Often in periods of sustained combat it was not always possible to apply to replacement vehicles the full range of vehicle markings and insignia. In this case, however, the crew have had time to apply the PL (Poland) sign and 52 (2nd Armoured Regiment identification number) on the left hand side of the tank, the triangle (indicating A Squadron) on the rear of the hull) and the Winged Hussar divisional insignia above the right-hand track. (AHA)

109. Artillery Bombardment, Normandy, August, 1944. Smoke rises from burning vehicles or buildings, the result of artillery bombardments on German positions to the front. The 1st Polish Armoured Division could call upon artillery support from its divisional artillery, the 1st and 2nd Field Artillery Regiments. One regiment deployed 24 Sexton self-propelled 25 pounder guns. The other regiment operated the towed version. The Poles could also call on artillery support from Canadian Medium Artillery Regiments with their more powerful and longer-ranged 5.5 inch medium guns. (PISM)

110. Battlegroup Advance, Normandy, August 1944. (Sequential photos 110-112). An all-arms battlegroup of tanks and armoured vehicles advance across an open field towards Falaise. On the horizon on the right of the photo can be seen a number of Sherman Vs, together with a Firefly with its distinctive long 17 pounder gun. Behind them are two Humber scout cars, for reconnaissance and liaison. The Sherman behind them may be that of the battlegroup commander. In the left foreground is a Bren-gun carrier taking advantage of the limited cover available. Entering the photo from the left are two Achilles self-propelled anti-tank guns (identified by the counter weight fitted immediately behind the muzzle-break). These are positioned ready to move forward help the forward Shermans in any encounter with the more powerful German tanks such as the Panther or Tiger. (PISM)

111. First Armoured Regiment, Normandy, 9th August, 1944. On the second day of Operation TOTALIZE, tanks from the 1st Armoured Regiment advance towards Hill 111 (military mapping practice identifies hills by their spot height). Note the Sherman in the centre with its turret rotated to the 3 o'clock position ensuring that all potential threats are covered.
Earlier "Worthington Force" (named after its commander Lieutenant Colonel Donald Worthington) a tank-infantry battlegroup from 4th Canadian Armoured Division had made a night-time advance to capture its own objective Point 195. Due to navigational errors the Canadians took the wrong route and established themselves on Hill 111 some distance from their intended objective, which was in fact a Polish one. Unfortunately it took some time before both "Worthington Force" and 4th Canadian Armoured Division realized the error. For the Germans, the location of "Worthington Force" posed a severe danger to their defensive positions and immediately attacked to remove this threat. (PISM)

112. First Armoured Regiment, Normandy, August 1944. Once the Poles became aware of the Canadian situation, they made every effort to relieve the beleaguered "Worthington Force". However the Germans redirected their fire onto these relief efforts. Some Polish tanks were able to get within 300 yards of the Canadians but, unsupported by infantry, suffered heavy losses, 22 tanks and 24 casualties. Major Aleksander Stefanowicz, commanding 1st Armoured Regiment saw no alternative but to withdraw and loaded his wounded on to his surviving tanks. Although seven Canadian Shermans were able to break-out to link up with the Poles, "Worthington Force" was almost totally annihilated and Colonel Worthington was killed. In this photo Shermans from the 1st Armoured Regiment move forward in the distance, almost certainly prior to the encounter with "Worthington Force". The armoured vehicle at the extreme left of the picture is one of the 1st Anti-Tank Regiment's M10/Achilles self-propelled anti-tank guns supporting the advance. (PISM)

113. Sherman tanks, Normandy, August 1944. A group of Sherman Vs from an unidentified Armoured Regiment move forward. The hot dry Normandy summer resulted in large clouds of dust accompanying any major vehicle movement. This reduced visibility and could also attract enemy artillery fire which could range on the clouds. The Sherman in the centre could be a Firefly with its long 17 pounder gun. (PISM).

114. Crusader Anti-Aircraft tank, Normandy, August, 1944. A Crusader Mk II/III Anti-Aircraft tank from the 24th *Uhlans* advances across rolling open country during Operation TOTALIZE. On its turret rear, partially obscured is the diamond shaped tactical marking showing that the vehicle is part of the regiment's headquarters squadron. To its left is a Humber Scout Car, probably also attached to the HQ Squadron for liaison duties. The Crusader is providing cover and is here supporting an advance by one of the 24th *Uhlans'* Squadrons. One platoon of Shermans has reached the crest of the hill (illustrating the dangers of being exposed against the horizon) while another platoon of tanks is moving up in support, below the crest. (PISM)

115. Sherman tanks, Normandy, 8th August 1944. Sherman Vs from the 3rd Squadron (circle on turret rear), the 24th *Uhlans*, the junior Armoured Regiment of the 1st Polish Armoured Division's, 10th Armoured Cavalry Brigade. More Shermans can be seen on the horizon. The tank on the right is taking advantage of the limited concealment offered by the rather small trees to its front. Both vehicle commanders, wearing the British Army tank crewman's protective helmet are seated low in their turrets thus protecting themselves, but still being in a position to observe the tactical situation and direct their vehicles. Both tanks mount 0.50 calibre machine guns on their turrets. The right hand tank has a small pennant flying from one of its radio aerials. In the Western Desert campaigns this was sometimes was used as a recognition element. The pennant being flown at a different height each day. It is impossible to say whether a similar practice is being employed here. (PISM)

116. Sherman tanks Normandy, August 1944. The Sherman shown in the previous image (with the pennant attached to its radio aerial) has moved forward. It appears to be providing cover for the Sherman Crab Mk I mine-clearing tank to its left. The Sherman Crab was a standard Sherman fitted with a forward mounted revolving drum, fitted with steel chain flails that beat the ground as the vehicle advanced exploding buried mines as it went. A single Crab could clear a single path eight-foot wide (see photo 122). When a minefield was discovered, two troops of Crabs (six tanks) would flail a lane 48-feet wide. Here the Crab has lowered its boom to the mine-clearing position. However its turret is still trained forward (when flailing the turret was rotated to the rear, to avoid damage to the gun). So in this case the Crab is probably being held in reserve. In the hedge at the left of the picture is an abandoned German Army IF8 (*Infanteriefahrzeug ausf 8*) cart. This was the most common German platoon supply/weapons cart in World War II. Interchangeable tow bars enabled it to be moved by a single horse, hand pulled or towed by a light vehicle such as a *Kettenkrad*, motorcycle combination or *Kübelwagen*. These carts were often linked in tandem. (PISM)

117. Sherman tanks, Normandy, August 1944. Surrounded by dust clouds three Shermans move forward. (PISM)

118. Firefly and Sherman tanks, Normandy, August 1944. A group of four Polish tanks halt during the advance. Two Sherman Vs are taking advantage of the tree cover on the right. The other two tanks in the photo have taken up a more defensive position. In the centre is another Sherman V. Beyond that is a Sherman Firefly with its long 17 pounder gun which made it a distinctive priority target for German gunners. Platoon commanders were therefore forbidden from using Fireflys as their command vehicle. (PISM)

119. Regiment Orders Group, Normandy, August 1944. Commanding Officers "O" (Orders) Group. Officers from Major Jan Kanski's, 24th *Uhlans*, confer with those of Lieutenant Colonel Wladyslaw Zgorzelski's, 10th Dragoons at the latter's command post. The 10th Dragoons was the integral motor battalion for the 3rd Armoured Cavalry Brigade. Note 10th Dragoons Command M5 half-track with its additional radio aerials and the raised cover over the rear of the vehicle to provide a suitable working area for officers and radio operators, and a 24th *Uhlans* Sherman V, either Major Kanski's command tank or one from his Regimental Headquarters. The extra "applique" armour seen on the side of the Sherman was intended to provide additional protection against enemy anti-tank weapons. Major Kanski (see photo 75) was mortally wounded at Jort, on 16 August 1944, during an artillery barrage and died in hospital 29 August 1944. On the 25 November 1944, he was posthumously promoted to Lieutenant Colonel. (PISM)

120. PaK 43 Ant-Tank Gun, Normandy, August, 1944. An abandoned 8.8cm, PaK (*PanzerabwehrKanone*) 43. Behind the gun is it's knocked out tractor, possibly a French *Souma* S 307. On the horizon centre is a Sexton self-propelled gun, while to the right of the picture, a Sherman Crab Mark I Flail mine-clearing tank, with its flail boom lowered moves forward. The PaK 43 was the German Army's most powerful towed anti-tank gun, entering service in 1943. It could penetrate all allied tanks at long ranges, even the Soviet IS-2 heavy tank on the Eastern Front. It was heavy and awkward to move without the aid of a tractor and as a result earned itself the nickname of "*Scheunentor*" (Barn Door) from its crews. (PISM)

121. Second Armoured Regiment Sherman tanks, Normandy, August 1944. A Sherman tank and its crew pause during the advance. One of the crew has dismounted while the others are observing the distant action. A spare track wheel is fixed next to the driver's position. Underneath that are a couple of spare track links. Compared to other nationalities the Poles were renowned for the neatness of external stowage on the exterior of their tanks. Below the right hand track-link on the front of the Sherman can be seen the divisional insignia of the "Winged Hussar". In the distance other Shermans continue the move forward. The lead tank may be a Firefly mounting the long 17 pounder. (PISM)

122. Sherman tanks, Normandy, August 1944. A column of Sherman tanks advance down a track. Probably this route has already been tested and cleared for mines as a number of markers have been placed along the edge of the track on the left hand side of the picture. Various methods were used by engineers to mark cleared paths though minefields, such as laying out mine tape formed from long strips of white cloth. The most effective method of clearing mine fields was the use of specially equipped Sherman Crab Flail Tanks (see photo 116). Flail tanks carried markers (as seen here) that could be placed along the cleared route and could be illuminated in conditions of low visibility or darkness. (PISM)

123. Sherman tank, Normandy, August 1944. A Sherman tank from "B" Squadron (square making on the turret rear) of an unidentified armoured regiment forces its way through a hedge. The hedgerows south of Caen were not on the same scale of the *bocage* elsewhere in Normandy, but could still present a formidable obstacle, as well as providing very effective concealment for German anti-tank teams. Note how the front of the tank is being raised as it moves forward. This could expose the very vulnerable belly of the vehicle to anti-tank weaponry. Elsewhere in Normandy the US Army had developed a special device named after its inventor "the Cullin Hedgerow Cutter" a series of metal spikes which, fitted to the front of a tank, enabled it to rapidly force its way through the hedge without exposure to enemy fire. (PISM)

124. Canadian Army Sherman, Normandy, August, 1944. A probable Canadian Army Sherman moves along a cleared route through a hedge. The 4th Canadian Armoured Division deployed to Normandy at the same time as the 1st Polish Armoured Division and both formed the key armoured elements in both Operation TOTALIZE and TRACTABLE. The crew of this Sherman have used sandbags to provide additional frontal protection against enemy tank and anti-tank guns. Usually ineffective, the practice was tolerated by their commanders as it helped maintain the morale of tank crews who, whether British, Polish or Canadian, shared a widespread belief that their tanks were very inferior, both in levels of protection and fire-power, in comparison with their opponents, particularly the powerful German Tigers and Panthers. A spare front sprocket appears to be welded to the hull side to add some additional armour protection? (PISM)

125. Armoured Regiment Headquarters, Normandy, August, 1944. Headquarters elements from an unidentified armoured regiment pause during the advance. This image has been taken some distance behind the lines as the vehicles are not tactically parked, i.e. dispersed with space between the vehicles to avoid unnecessary casualties from shell-fire. Parked next to the Sherman is a Humber Scout car, nine of which served in the Liaison Platoon of each Armoured Regiment. Next to it are two M5 half-tracks serving as armoured ambulances with Red Cross identification symbols on their fronts and sides. (PISM)

126. Six Pounder Anti-tank gun, Normandy, August, 1944. A Canadian crew of a 6 pounder anti-tank gun struggle to bring it into action. It has just been unlimbered from its Loyd carrier tow. The Ordnance Quick-Firing 6 pounder 7 cwt was the standard British Army battalion level anti-tank gun from 1942 onwards equipping the anti-tank platoon in all British, Polish and Canadian infantry and motor battalions. It was not an easy task to manhandle it into position, as can be seen here by the efforts here of its crew. (PISM)

127. Loyd carriers, Normandy, August, 1944. Two Loyd carriers, having unlimbered the 6 pounder anti-tank guns they were towing (one of which is shown in the previous image), quickly relocate as the guns prepare for action. The Loyd was a 4.5 ton tracked vehicle used for a wide variety of tasks. In this particular role it is acting as the towing vehicle and crew transport for the 6 pounder anti-tank gun. Note Allied recognition star is at an angle, repositioned by the Canadians to distinguish their vehicles from those of their American and British Allies.(PISM)

128. Tiger Tank, Quesnay Woods Normandy, August, 1944. Polish soldiers closely examine a knocked out Pzkw VI Tiger tank in the vicinity of Quesnay Woods. The Tiger was regarded by Allied tank crews as the most formidable German tank opposing them in Normandy, although the total deployed in three heavy tank battalions never exceeded 150 vehicles. The Tiger's powerful High Velocity (HV) 88mm KwK (*KampfwagenKanone*) 36 could destroy Sherman and Cromwell tanks beyond the effective range of their own MV 75mm gun. However the Tiger was not totally invulnerable, as this Tiger from *schwere SS-Panzerabteilung 101* (1st Heavy SS Tank Battalion), was knocked out by a Cromwell from 10th Mounted Rifles. It was also mechanically unreliable. A Centaur Mk II/III Anti-Aircraft Gun tank is s pulled up alongside. Quesnay Wood was a significant Allied objective, heavily defended by the Germans. Efforts to capture it by the Canadians on 10 August failed and was one of the factors that caused Lieutenant General Simonds to call-off Operation TOTALIZE the following day. (PISM)

129. German PoWs, Jort, Normandy, 15 August 1944. German soldiers, their hands in the air to indicate surrender, move past advancing Polish forces in the vicinity of Jort. These soldiers, are probably from the *85. Infanteriedivsion*, who defended Jort and who's *Pioneerkompanie* were able to destroy the bridges over the River Dives before the Poles could capture them. (PISM)

130. StuG III, Normandy, August 1944. A destroyed German StuG III G assault gun. About 550 were deployed in Normandy. Originally designed as an infantry close-support vehicle it became increasing used as a tank-destroyer as the war progressed, especially when fitted with a long 7.5cm StuK 40 gun. The roof of this vehicle's fighting compartment has been blown off, either by bombs or artillery or an internal explosion. The bent metal rail just above the track supported the steel side skirts known as *Schurzen*, originally fitted to defeat Soviet anti-tank rifles. Spare road wheels are carried on the rear of the vehicle. Its low profile, which made detection difficult, made it ideally suited to its defensive role in Normandy. It was deployed in panzer and infantry divisions and independent assault gun units. (PISM)

131. Normandy, August 1944. Two Polish soldiers seek shelter under a half-track. They and their fellow crew-members have dug out a trench over which the vehicle has been moved to provide protection against enemy air attack or more likely artillery bombardment. Both are wearing RAC protective helmets, and may be the vehicle crew. These soldiers and their half-track are from the 24th *Uhlans* light aid detachment. In the distance is a Sherman ARV (armoured recovery vehicle). One ARV was attached to each armoured squadron. (PISM)

132. Sexton Self-propelled gun, Normandy, August 1944. A Sexton self-propelled gun from the Polish Armoured Division's 1st Motorised Artillery Regiment in action. The 25 pounder self-propelled, tracked, Sexton was a Canadian conversion of their indigenous tank design, the Ram, which never entered service as a gun-tank. It was adapted to mount the standard British Army 25 pounder field gun (see photo 67). The Sexton served in one of the two Artillery Regiments (each with 24 guns) in all British, Polish and Canadian Armoured Divisions. In front of the Sexton is a M5 half-track which may be serving as a battery command post coordinating the fire of its eight guns. (PISM)

133. *Waffen-SS* prisoner, Normandy, 22-24 August, 1944. Colonel Franciszek Skibiński, (left) deputy commander 10th Armoured Cavalry Brigade observes the interrogation of a captured *Waffen-SS Panzergrenadier* (identified by the *Waffen-SS* decal on his helmet and by his lapel badges). This *SS-Schütze* (private) is from *12.SS-Panzerdivision*, perhaps may be from *SS-Panzergrenadierregiment 25* (see photo 142) which as part of *Kampfgruppe Waldmuller* was in action with the Poles during the opening stages of Operation TOTALIZE. Round his neck is the single piece *Erkennungsmarke* (identity disc) as used by all branches of the German Armed Forces. Behind Colonel Skibinski, the commander of a Humber scout car consults a map in a protective map case. In the background is a M5 half-track. (PISM)

134. German Army prisoners, Normandy, 8 August 1944. German Army Prisoners, one of whom is perhaps wounded, move towards the rear. The soldiers may be from the *89. Infanteriedivision* which had only occupied its front-line positions a day or so before the start of TOTALIZE. The division had been formed in February 1944 and had come to France from Norway in June. It was known as the "Horseshoe Division" (based on its unit insignia). The soldier on the left may be holding a *Passierschein* (safe conduct pass) an Alllied propaganda leaflet intended to persuade German soldiers to surrender. In the background is a probable M10/Achilles self-propelled anti-tank gun, alongside it there appears to be a towed 17 pounder. Further along the hedge to the right is a Sherman. In the distance are two M5 half-tracks used by the Armoured Brigade's Motor Battalion, a version of the M3 half-track solely allocated to the Lend-Lease programme. (PISM)

135. German PoWs, Normandy, August 1944. Scottish soldiers from 51st Highland Division escort two groups of captured Germans to the rear areas where they will be held in temporary PoW Cages for interrogation and processing before being sent on to PoW camps either in the United Kingdom, the United States or Canada. A guard wearing a Scottish bonnet brings up the rear of the column. The prisoners appear to be from the *Heer* (Army) rather than *Waffen-SS*. The 51st Highland Division formed part of II Canadian Corps for Operation TOTALIZE. On the horizon at the extreme left of the picture is the distinctive silhouette of a Sherman Firefly, with its long 17 pounder and rear-turret extension, demonstrating the vulnerability of Allied armour advancing across such open spaces against concealed German tanks, self-propelled guns and anti-tank guns. (PISM)

136. *Passierschein*, **Normandy, August 1944**. Allied psychological warfare leaflet, his example coloured in pink hue. The front of an Allied "Safe-Conduct" pass, (see photo 134) promising German soldiers who surrendered good and fair treatment. These leaflets could either be distributed from aircraft or fired in special shells. Intended to encourage German soldiers to desert, they were mainly directed at those members of the German army of doubtful allegiance and who had been conscripted into the German Army as a result of their countries' incorporation, with varying degrees of enthusiasm, into the Reich, such as Austrians, Czechs and Poles. The penalties for deserters, and their families were severe. If found, such leaflets could not be picked up by anyone below the rank of major. To be found in un-authorised possession would certainly have resulted in execution. (AHA)

Auf Grund von Kapitel 2, Artikel 11, Vertragsnummer 846 der Genfer Konvention vom 27. Juli 1929 erhalten kriegsgefangene Soldaten* in amerikanischen oder britischen Händen die gleiche Verpflegung wie Soldaten des amerikanischen oder britischen Heeres. Ihr Essen wird von Köchen aus ihren eigenen Reihen auf die Art ihres Landes zubereitet.

In Amerika oder Kanada erhalten Kriegsgefangene für ihre Arbeit innerhalb oder außerhalb des Lagers pro Tag 80 cents.   Die Hälfte davon wird für die Zeit nach dem Krieg auf einer Bank hinterlegt, die andere Hälfte in Gutscheinen ausgezahlt, mit denen sich der Gefangene Marketenderwaren wie Zigaretten, Süßigkeiten, alkoholfreie Getränke und dergleichen kaufen kann.

Den Kriegsgefangenen wird Gelegenheit geboten zur Abhaltung von Bildungs- und Lehrkursen, zur Ausübung von Sport und Spielen und zur Veranstaltung von Konzerten, Theateraufführungen und Vorträgen.   Sie dürfen Zeitungen lesen und Rundfunk hören.

Postverbindung zwischen den Gefangenenlagern und der Heimat geht über das Rote Kreuz. Sie ist zuverlässig und verhältnismäßig schnell. Nach Kriegsende werden die Gefangenen so bald wie möglich nach Hause zurückgeschickt.

*Als Soldaten werden auf Grund der Haager Konvention (IV. 1907) angesehen: Alle bewaffneten Personen, die Uniform tragen oder ein Abzeichen, das von einer Entfernung aus erkannt werden kann.

ZG 37

137. *Passierschein*, Normandy, August 1944. Reverse side. (AHA)

138. Mortar team, Normandy, August 1944. Two Polish mortar teams from either an infantry or motor battalion prepare their weapons for firing. The support company of each British, Polish or Canadian infantry battalion and motor battalion included a mortar platoon equipped with six × 3 inch mortars, providing a battalion with its own indirect fire support. The mortar could fire both high-explosive and smoke rounds to a range of 1,600 yards and had a maximum rate of fire of about 15 rounds a minute. It could be broken down into three man-portable loads, barrel, bipod and baseplate, and could be transported in a Bren or Universal carrier. Each mortar was served by a three-man crew. Because of the summer heat some members of both crews have removed their battledress jackets. A Sherman tank can be seen in the distance. (PISM)

139. Six pounder anti-tank gun, Normandy, August 1944. A Polish six pounder anti-tank and crew prepare for action. The support company of each British, Polish or Canadian infantry or motor battalion included a six gun strong antitank platoon equipped with six pounder anti-tank guns. The Ordnance Quick-Firing 6-pounder was the standard British Army battalion level anti-tank gun from 1942 onwards, equipping the anti-tank platoon in all British, Polish and Canadian infantry and motor battalions. It had an effective range of 1,093 yards and a rate of fire of 15 rounds per minute. Here the 6 pounder has been sited behind cover so that only its barrel is exposed. The soldier wearing the Royal Armoured Corps rimless helmet, as opposed to the Mark II Steel Helmet worn by the gun crew (six men), may be the driver of the Loyd Carrier tow. The ropes on the gun shield could be used to help drag or tow the gun into position. (PISM)

140. Stuarts and Achilles, Normandy, August 1944. A column of two Stuart Mk V light tanks move forward, with some probably concealed in the distant dust clouds. The "A" on the rear turret of the last vehicle in the column is probably that vehicle's call sign. The white tapes probably indicate the border of a mine-cleared track. Further up the columns is a M10/Achilles self-propelled anti-tank gun with is barrel reversed. This may be present to provide support should the Stuart encounter opposition. (PISM)

141. German PoWs, Normandy, August 1944. A group of German PoWs, who appear to be from the *Heer* move past two Polish Humber scout cars on their way to a Prisoner-of-War cage. (PISM)

142. *Waffen-SS* prisoner, Normandy, August, 1944. A *Waffen-SS Panzergrenadier* is taken into captivity by a delighted Polish soldier. He is from the *12. SS-Panzerdivision Hitler Jugend* which formed the core of the German defence against the Poles and Canadians during Operations TOTALIZE and TRACTABLE and may also be from *SS-Panzergrenadierregiment 25*, part of *Kampfgruppe Waldmuller* (see photo 133). He is wearing the distinctive camouflage pattern uniform issued solely to the *Waffen-SS*. The *12. SS-Panzer Division Hitler Jugend* had been raised in 1943 from 18 year-old members of the Hitler Youth, with a cadre of experienced officers and NCOs from *1. SS-Panzerdivision Leibstandarte Adolf Hitler* and had been engaged in almost continuous combat in Normandy since 7 July. It had suffered heavy losses (reduced from over 20,000 personal to around 11,000-11,500 at the time of TOTALIZE). (PISM)

143. Burnt-out Sherman, Normandy, August 1944. A knocked-out Sherman V. It has lost its right-hand track, and the discolourisation along its side might be evidence of internal fire. There are no visible markings. British tank crews blamed the propensity for Shermans to burst into flames, when hit, on their petrol engines. In fact this was due to the vulnerability of the Sherman to ammunition fires. On the side of this vehicle can be seen two applique armour plates designed to increase protection levels for the on-board ammunition. However operational research carried out by 21st Army Group could find no recorded example where these applique plates had worked. In fact it was felt that these plates only served as aiming marks for German gunners. (PISM)

144. German Self-propelled Gun, Normandy, August 1944. Polish soldiers inspect an unidentified German armoured vehicle. The gun would appear to be a 150mm sFH 18/L30 howitzer, the same as that mounted on the SdKfz 165 *Hummel* self-propelled gun, but appears to be in different position from the mounting on that vehicle. If any reader is able to positively identify this "mystery" vehicle, please e-mail the publisher. (PISM)

145. Knocked out Shermans and Fireflys, the *Maczuga*, Normandy, August 1944. Knocked out Polish tanks. The tanks on the right and left are Sherman Vs with the 75mm gun. The two in the centre are 17 pounder equipped Fireflys. All have their barrels pointed to the direction from which they were attacked. (PISM)

146. Knocked out Sherman, the *Maczuga*, Normandy, August 1944. A close-up of the tank shown on the right of the previous photo. The tank is a Sherman V named "Barfly". The bodies of its dead crew lie beside it. (PISM)

147. Knocked-out StuG III, Normandy, August, 1944. A knocked-out/abandoned StuG III. The *Saukopf* ('pigs-head") mantlet identifies it as a late production model. The raised panel above the gun is not a hatch, but a shield for a dismountable machine-gun (MG-34 or MG-42) that could be fired by the vehicle's loader as a secondary weapon. (PISM)

148. 10th Dragoons, Normandy, August, 1944. Infantry from the 10th Dragoons move forward along a ditch running by a muddy road. A Sherman can be partly seen on the left of the picture, providing support. At full strength an infantry section at this time would consist of about ten men armed with Sten Guns, rifles and a Bren Gun. Casualities invariably would quickly reduce this number. Serving in the Armoured Brigade's Motor Battalion these infantry would normally be transported in carriers or M5 Armoured half-tracks, but would normally dismount to go into action. Several appear to be wearing the Tankers helmet, including the soldier, third from the right.(PISM)

149. Polish Infantry, Normandy, August 1944. Polish soldiers from an unidentified infantry or motor battalion take cover along a hedgerow. They have dug foxholes for themselves which will provide some protection from shell and mortar fire. The weather in Normandy was hot and the soldiers seen here are either wearing an army issue 'cap comforter' (foreground) or a bandanas under their Mk II steel helmets to keep sweat out of their eyes. The soldier in the centre may be an NCO as, in front of him, is a Mk III 9mm Sten submachine gun It was cheap to manufacture and was produced in large quantities, although in service it had performance and reliability issues (such as firing when the safety was "on")! (PISM)

150. Polish Infantry Company HQ Normandy, August 1944. Elements of an infantry company HQ dug-in along a hedgerow with a Wireless Set No 18 radio. It had a range of about five miles and was used as a link between battalion and company headquarters. It could be man-packed by its operator, the soldier in the centre, who is holding a microphone in his left hand and could be wearing headphones under his steel helmet. The other two soldiers are probably also part of the company HQ. The soldier on the left has acquired a German MP 40 sub-machine gun. To the right a soldier mans a Bren gun. This very effective .303-calibre, light machine gun was fed from a distinctive curved 30 round magazine, with a rate of fire of 120 rounds a minute. It was issued on the basis of one per infantry-section, and would also have been available to the company HQ for defence. (PISM)

151. Wounded German PoWs, **Normandy, August 1944**. A wounded German prisoner (see also photo 152) is attended to by a Polish soldier who may have provided the cigarettes. Once treated the soldier and his comrades will be moved to PoW handling facilities in the rear. By this stage of the War Allied medical services were so superior to those of the Germans, that these prisoners will be receiving a much higher standard of medical treatment than could be provided by their own medical units. (PISM)

152. Wounded German PoW, **Normandy, August 1944**. The Polish soldier finishes his treatment of the wounded PoW (see photo 151), while an unwounded German soldier looks on. Both appear older than the average front-line German soldier and may be from a second-line or administrative unit. They may have only recently been called-up, as Germany was forced to commit more and more of its available manpower to its armed forces, employing women and slave labourers in vital industries and services to release men to the front. (PISM)

153. Prisoner of War processing, Normandy, August 1944. A large group of German captured soldiers being processed while under guard by a Polish soldier with a Vickers K machine gun mounted on a 2nd Armoured Regiment Humber scout car with its "53" (24th Lancers) Arm of Service Number on its rear. Note also the handwritten "PL" a nationality plate. The PoWs at the front of the line seem to have their hands over their head and are probably being searched for documents or questioned for any information that might be of immediate intelligence value. Also the Poles might be trying to identify fellow countrymen who have been conscripted into the German Army and who now may wish to join the 1st Polish Armoured Division. (PISM)

154. Casualties, Normandy, August 1944. Normandy, August 1944. Polish soldiers from an unidentified armoured regiment attend to battlefield casualties. One is being attended to in the ditch at the right by some tank crewmen. Of the two soldiers squatting to the left of the picture, the one on the right is a motorcycle dispatch rider while the partly hidden figure would appear to be another armoured soldier. On the rear of the despatch rider's helmet is a number, perhaps his unit's Arm of Service number. He is wearing a German pistol holster. A Webley pistol is visible in the holster on the soldier to his left. One of the three soldiers in the top-hand left corner of the photo appears to be wearing a medical brassard. A Sherman tank can be seen moving along the road in the background. (PISM)

155. German Propaganda, Warsaw, 16 June, 1944. The Poles learn of D-Day. The front page of the edition of *Nowy Kurier Warszawski* (New Courier of Warsaw) for 16 June 1944. When the Germans occupied Poland they closed all existing newspapers and replaced them with their own Polish-language titles such as this, in order to disseminate their version of events to the Poles. This front page shows the German propaganda view of D-Day and is designed to impress upon readers a narrative of German success and Allied defeat and is headed by pictures from still and newsreel footage taken very soon after D-Day. The left hand image shows a *12.SS Panzerdivision* MG-42 gunner. The centre photo shows a *Waffen-SS* soldier examining a knocked out Canadian Sherman, his recently acquired Bren-gun carrier alongside him. The final image shows a bombed-out street in Caen. A reminder to the Poles of what liberation by their allies could actually mean. (AHA)

156. "Eighty-eight", Normandy, August 1944. A Polish tank crewman (wearing the distinctive rimless helmet) carrying a Sten sub-machine gun examines an abandoned/knocked-out German 8.8 cm Flak (*Flugzeugabwehrkanone*) 36 anti-aircraft gun. This gun has been deployed in the anti-tank role in which it was very effective. It had a range of some 16,250 yards and could destroy any Allied armoured vehicle. Its height made it difficult to conceal and here a limited effort has been made to camouflage this particular gun. The crew were also vulnerable to artillery fire. In Normandy "eight-eights" were widely deployed. A number of German formations encountered by the Poles during Operation TOTALIZE used this gun, in particular *SS-Flakabteilung 12* of the *12. SS-Panzerdivision* and also in the combined anti-tank and anti-aircraft regiment of *89. Infanteriedivision*. Also facing the Poles and Canadians were elements of the Luftwaffe's *III FlakKorp*. The role of this formation was primarily air defence but deployed some of its 8.8 cm Flak guns against enemy armour during Operation TOTALIZE. (PISM)

157. Normandy, August 1944. A Panther *ausfuhrung* A abandoned in a Normandy farmyard. It is estimated that of the 2,336 tanks, assault guns and tank destroyers the German deployed in Normandy around 1,500 were lost (destroyed or abandoned) during the campaign. Lying In the foreground are various discarded items of military equipment.(PISM)

158. Advanced Landing Ground (ALG) B-10, Plumetot, Normandy, August 1944. Three Polish Spitfire IXs at readiness on ALG B-10 at Plumetot. The machine on the right, with the squadron identification code JH-V is from 317 (Wilno) Polish Fighter Squadron. On 3 August 1944, 131 (Polish) Wing flew to France. Conditions at Plumetot were very difficult. The strip was still in a range of German artillery and the air and ground-crew had to stay in ad-hoc shelters. During hot days dust covered everything and turned to mud after it rained. At night the constant din of artillery fire (from both sides) made rest almost impossible. (PISM)

159. Advanced Landing Ground (ALG) B-10, Plumetot, Normandy, August 1944. Polish ground crew secure a bomb to a Spitfire IX, from 131 (Polish) Wing. The aircraft wears standard RAF camouflage and markings, but with Polish national insignia on its nose, beneath the exhaust. Under the port wing the Allied Air Forces stripped black/white recognition marking can be seen. Polish airmen wore RAF uniform but with Polish insignia. The figure in the centre, by the 20mm wing mounted cannon, may well be the pilot. He is wearing flying boots, with maps or charts stuffed into the one on his left leg. Pilots flew many sorties each day, attacking enemy troops, transport, artillery positions and supply depots. The Spitfire IX was fitted with a 500 pound bomb rack under its belly and 250 pound racks under each wing. Here a 500 pound general purpose bomb is being fitted for a ground attack mission. (PISM)

160. Advanced Landing Ground (ALG) B-10, Plumetot, Normandy, August 1944. A Polish Spitfire IX at dispersal. ALG B-10 at Plumetot, to the north of Caen was built during June by 25th Airfield Construction Group, Royal Engineers, part of an extensive airfield building programme in the bridgehead. Spitfires from 131 (Polish) Wing were based here between August-September 1944 with aircraft flying both air defence and ground support operations. At the time the Wing comprised 302 (City of Poznan) Polish Fighter Squadron, 308 (City of Krakow) Polish Fighter Squadron and 317 (Wilno) Polish Fighter Squadron. (PISM). A Norman farmer goes about his regular agricultural tasks nearby. (PISM)

Part IV
The *Maczuga* and Chambois
16-21 August 1944

During the progress of Operations TOTALIZE and TRACTABLE dramatic developments on the US front would now have a decisive impact on the future operations of the 1st Polish Armoured Division.

To the west, Operation COBRA, the US Army's break-out offensive launched from the direction of Saint Lo on 25 July, after an indifferent start was now making impressive progress and the German left wing appeared to be facing imminent collapse as American armoured units advanced southwards towards Brittany. At this stage Adolf Hitler took charge. From his study of maps in his command bunker in far-away East Prussia he ordered a counter-attack with the intention of isolating the American spearheads and reversing the course of the campaign. To achieve this he ordered the transfer of as many *panzer* divisions as could be spared from those forces facing the British and Canadians. His generals thought the plan stood little chance but, in the light of the recent failed assassination attempt on the life of the *Fuhrer* they felt they had little choice but to carry out their orders. So on 7 August, the same day that TOTALIZE began, the Germans launched their counter-attack codenamed LUTTICH. The German assault at Mortain achieved some initial surprise and early success, thanks to the presence of early morning mist. But as this dispersed, Allied fighter bombers in strength appeared over the German *panzer* columns, subjecting them to heavy attack. Despite lack of progress Hitler ordered the attacks to continue for a second day, seemingly unaware of the danger his actions were threatening to his armies in Normandy.

In contrast this was seen as an opportunity by both General Montgomery and General Bradley. On 8 August it was decided that the 1st US Army and 3rd US Army would swing north towards Flers and Argentan. With the 2nd British and 1st Canadian Armies pushing down from the North, the German armies in Normandy, 7.*Armee* and 5. *Panzerarmee* could be trapped and annihilated.

To achieve this it would be necessary to capture a number of key locations on the routes that would be available to the Germans should they decide to retreat. These were the towns of Falaise, Trun, Chambois, Vimoutiers and Argentan. On the 11 August Montgomery ordered that "Canadian Army will capture Falaise. This is a first priority, and it is vital it should be done quickly". It was then to move south to Argentan to link up with the 3rd US Army.

General Crerar on 15 August instructed General Simonds that as soon as Falaise had been taken, he was to direct his two armoured divisions on Trun. General Maczek had been unhappy at the restricted frontages his division had been ordered to adopt for TOTALIZE and had seen the possibilities for manoeuvre by attacking eastward, and had ordered his staff to develop plans for such an eventuality. It has been suggested that Maczek may have drawn Simonds' attention to the possibilities of such an action. Whatever the inspiration, General Simonds came to a momentous decision. He ordered Maczek to swing away from the main line of II Canadian Corps advance and head towards Trun. As a first objective 1st Polish Armoured Division was to seize a bridgehead over the River Dives. It was an impressive example of the trust General Simonds had in the Polish Armoured Division and its commander to carry out this task. On 15 August, moving in advance of the main body of the division, a battlegroup led by Major Jan Maciejowski, the 10th Mounted Rifles commanding officer (who had been wounded the day before when his tank ran over a mine) advanced towards Jort to seize bridges over the River Dives. His force comprised his own Cromwell-equipped divisional armoured reconnaissance regiment, a company of motorised infantry from the 10th Dragoons (the armoured brigade's motor rifle battalion) in half-tracks and carriers, a battery of 17 pounder Achilles self-propelled anti-tank guns from the divisional anti-tank regiment (to make up for the lack of Fireflys in the 10th Mounted Rifles). The 5.5 inch guns of a Canadian medium artillery regiment would provide fire support. Like many river obstacles in Normandy, the Dives was quite narrow, but with steep banks which, in the absence of bridges, required engineering effort to span them.

At Jort one Cromwell squadron cleared the approaches to the town of defenders who were supported by three anti-tank guns, while infantry moved into the town to seize the bridges. During the action the Poles were counter-attacked by a small number of Tigers, which were driven off by fire from the anti-tank battery's Achilles and the guns of the supporting Canadian artillery, but with the loss of two Polish tanks with three more damaged. One of the Tigers was captured intact.

Despite this, the German defenders, a *Pioneerkompanie* from 85. *Infanteriedivision*, were able to destroy the bridges. However a Polish patrol captured a group of *Osttruppen* (units formed by the Germans from former Soviet PoWs recruited into the German Army, usually in the hope of better living conditions) who revealed the existence of a ford capable of supporting armoured vehicles. Two tanks crossed the river, while a further six were towed across by steel cables. This enabled the Poles to launch an attack into the German rear resulting in the capture of the town. The Poles had lost three tanks, with five damaged. While waiting for Bailey pre-fabricated bridging equipment to be brought forward, Polish sappers were able to construct, in 4 ½ hours a temporary bridge over which some 400 vehicles were able to cross before daylight on the 16 August (in pre-invasion exercises in the United Kingdom 1st Polish Armoured Division had been commended for their river crossing operations). During the night the bridgehead was bombed. The next morning Focke-Wulf 190 aircraft attacked the headquarters units established around the bridgehead inflicting casualties in a rare daylight appearance by the *Luftwaffe*. Unfortunately during the day the commanding officer of the 24th *Uhlans*, Major Jan Witold Kanski was mortally wounded at Jort, during an artillery barrage and died in hospital 29 August 1944.

On 16 August following urgent appeals from his senior Army commanders in Normandy, *SS-Oberstgruppenfuhrer* Hausser of the 7.*Armee* and *General* Eberbach of 5.*Panzerarmee*, *Generalfeldmarschall* Gunter Von Kluge, the overall German Commander in the West, was able, with a reluctant *Fuhrer*'s approval, to order a retreat. German forces now began a difficult withdrawal from Normandy down a rapidly decreasing number of routes, that the Allies were now making strenuous efforts to close.

Following the heavy fighting after D-Day the commanders of the British Armoured Divisions (Guards, 7th and 11th) deployed to Normandy in 21st Army Group found that the organisation of their formations was not particularly suitable for the tactical situation in which they found themselves. The nature of the terrain and strength and depth of the German defences necessitated greater co-operation between infantry and armour. Therefore, rather than having separate armoured and infantry brigades their headquarters would command mixed groupings of armoured regiments and infantry battalions, permitting much closer tank-infantry co-operation than before. It was similar in concept, but perhaps not as flexible as the German *kampfgruppe*. For the rest of the campaign Maczek also organised his division into all-arms battlegroups. How much this was the result of Maczek's analysis of the lessons of the campaign, and how much he was influenced by the experience of the 21st Army Group's other armoured divisions is difficult to ascertain. Before the 1st Polish Armoured Division deployed, General Maczek sent two of his principal staff officers and a British liaison officer to Normandy to learn of fighting conditions there and to liaise with 11th Armoured Division. Unfortunately his Chief of Staff, Colonel Jerzy Levittoux, and Major William Willis, a British Liaison Officer, were killed in a German air-raid on 18 July.

Once across the River Dives Maczek organised his battlegroups around his four armoured units – 1st and 2nd Armoured Regiments, 24th *Uhlans* and 10th Mounted Rifles. Although the exact composition of each would change from time to time over the following days the core armoured element was supported by infantry from both the motor battalion and the 3rd Polish Infantry Brigade (*3 Brygada Strzelcow*),either in carriers or lorries, attached towed anti-tank guns (6 pounder and 17 pounder) and Bofors and Crusader anti-aircraft guns.

During the course of the 16 August Polish battlegroups moved out of the bridgehead.

However on 17 August 1st Polish Armoured's objectives changed again. General Montgomery ordered at 1445 hours that:

> It is absolutely essential that…both…4 Cdn Div and 1 Pol Armd Div close the gap between First Cdn Army and Third US Army. 1 Pol Armd Div must thrust on past TRUN to CHAMBOIS at all costs, and as quickly as possible.

Montgomery's order was personally communicated to General Maczek by Lieutenant General Simonds himself, emphasising its importance. Maczek received this order in his Cromwell tank in the Jort bridgehead. His preferred command style was to be as far forward as possible, directing operations from his command tank.

Although Montgomery's orders had specified the objective of the 1st Polish Armoured Division as Chambois, Maczek, an expert map-reader (a skill developed during his service with the Austro-Hungarian Army as a mountain infantryman, where the swift interpretation of contour lines was of vital tactical importance), had already identified two hills on a ridge-line running north-south between the River Dives and the town of Vimoutiers to the north of Chambois, above the village of Coudehard. Mazcek saw these hills, marked on military mapping (by their height) as Hills 262N and 262S, as vital objectives, both to support the defence of Chambois and interdict the routes that would be used by the retreating Germans. He also noticed that the contour lines on this area of high ground resembled the outlines of a medieval Polish weapon – a *Maczuga* (Mace), thus conferring the distinctive name by which this defensive position would be remembered. As they moved towards their objectives Maczek's battlegroups found themselves moving across the German line of retreat, as enemy forces struggled to avoid the closing Allied pincers. Collisions between the retreating Germans and advancing Poles were inevitable resulting in fierce, but often brief fire-fights, with not only the Germans, but the Poles also suffering casualties. As the 20th Mounted Rifles advanced near Trun it encountered a German column. Although the German force was quickly destroyed it cost a Polish armoured squadron all but two of its tanks with seven killed and 16 wounded. On another occasion in the dark, a German *Feldgendarme* (military policeman) waved on 2nd Armoured Regiment, their identity unrecognised, holding back two German columns, all bypassing without incident!

The country was hilly, and forested with narrow twisting roads making navigation difficult. Moving through the night, the column of Colonel Koszutski's 2nd Armoured Regiment lost its way and in the early morning found itself misdirected by a French guide to Les Champeaux, not Chambois, where they overran the HQ of the 2. *SS-Panzerdivision Das Reich.* After heavy fighting the Germans retreated leaving the Poles to examine the looted items the Germans had abandoned. To get themselves back on route the Poles enlisted the aid of another local guide but he was killed a short time later. Other Polish units also made contact with French resistance fighters, receiving varying degrees of assistance. The Polish columns were followed by supply convoys who endeavoured to keep the battlegroups supplied with fuel and ammunition. However time was vital and there was little time for rest as the Poles moved through the night, with infantrymen clinging to the sides of the tanks, as sometimes the battlegroups were forced to sacrifice resupply for speed of advance. As they fought their way through pockets of resistance, the Poles were hampered more by attacks by allied aircraft mistaking their columns for retreating Germans, which cost them casualties as well as valuable supplies of ammunition and fuel (on one such occasion a 2nd Armoured Regiment fuel convoy lost half of its load). Between 16-18 August, 72 Polish soldiers were killed and 191 wounded by these airstrikes. By this time Polish casualties made up 50% of those of II Canadian Corps, 263 compared with 286 (for three divisions and two brigades).

In the early morning of 19 August 1944, the tank crews of the 1st Armoured Regiment, together with two companies of the Polish *Podhale* Mountain Battalion (*Batalion Strzelcow Podhalanski*) were preparing for breakfast when a message was received from Brigade Headquarters ordering them to move to the *Maczuga*. The tank crews and soldiers were tired and hungry. The route they had been forced to take was difficult and hilly, there had been clashes with the enemy with little chance to eat hot meals and rest. During pauses in the advance the priority had been on servicing and maintaining their vehicles and weapons.

Advancing from the north towards their objectives, Hills 262N and 262S, the Poles encountered some Germans preparing defensive positions, who were promptly disarmed by the infantry of the *Podhale* Battalion. With the 1st Squadron providing cover, the 2nd Squadron moved towards Hill 262S. As they approached this objective the Poles encountered a retreating German column, consisting of a mixture of marching infantry, wheeled and horse-drawn transport, together with some Panther tanks. Strung along the road the German convoy presented an easy target for the Polish tanks who deployed in combat formation, and aided by the higher elevation of their position immediately opened a furious and devastating fire at point blank range. Their fire lasted about half an hour, the tanks of the 3rd Squadron expending all their main armament ammunition during the action. The result was a tangled mass of wreckage, many German and some Polish casualties and large haul of enemy PoWs. With the road now blocked, the Poles abandoned their move towards 262S and fell back, consolidating around 262N.

At 17.50 hours a battlegroup of tanks from the 2nd Armoured Regiment and 8th Infantry Battalion arrived (having been delayed by their unintended detour to Champeaux). In the early evening the remaining elements of the *Podhale* Battalion and the 9th Polish Infantry Battalion (less one company) also joined the battlegroup. By midnight, with the appearance of the missing infantry company, together with towed anti-tank guns and tracked anti-aircraft tanks, the force occupying the *Maczuga* was complete. The complete battlegroup now consisted of two armoured regiments and three infantry battalions, approximately 1,500-2,000 men and some 80-90 tanks. Suffering from only sporadic mortar fire during the night, the Poles prepared their defences.

Earlier, during the late afternoon of 19 August the Cromwells of 10th Mounted Rifle Regiment approached Chambois from the north-east. The tanks advanced cautiously, looking out for the Americans approaching from the south. In fact the first contact was with a German motor-cycle combination which was quickly despatched, and the Cromwells opened fire on German columns observed approaching Chambois. An urgent message from divisional headquarters warned of an imminent airstrike and air recognition panels were quickly displayed on the vehicles as waves of allied fighter-bombers pounded the town for an hour, filling the streets with destroyed vehicles. With the Cromwells providing covering fire from Hill 113 to the north-west of Chambois, the Sherman tanks of the 24th *Uhlans* and the infantry of the 10th Dragoons, mounted in their carriers, advanced into the town. Finding it impossible to move through the clogged streets, the infantry had to move through gardens and orchards, dealing both with enemy resistance and a growing number of enemy PoWs. On the southern edge of the town troops from his 3rd Squadron, 10th Dragoons reported to Second Lieutenant Jan Karcz that enemy reinforcements were approaching and fire was exchanged. However examining the approaching "enemy" through his binoculars, Karcz realised that they were wearing American uniforms. He placed his British-issue steel helmet on the end of a rifle and waved at the advancing infantry. Captain L.E. Waters greeted Lieutenant Karcz with the words "Glad to see you buddy". Contact had been made between the two allied pincers at 19.00 hours on 19 August.

The US infantry were G Company, 359th Infantry Regiment, 90th Division who, as they moved into the town found it absolutely devastated, the streets littered with destroyed or abandoned vehicles and German dead.

The Americans and Poles set about co-ordinating their joint defence of the captured town. The 359th Infantry Regiment supported by tanks and tank destroyers took responsibility for the southern area of Chambois, with the Poles from the 24th *Uhlans* and 10th Dragoons taking the north side, while the tanks of the 10th Mounted Rifles remained in their positions on Hill 113, supported by towed anti-tank guns. By now, after two weeks of intensive operations the Poles were in a critical supply state with serious shortages of fuel and ammunition. However 90th Infantry was in contact with its logistic support and was able to provide fuel and tank ammunition, which was vital to keep the Poles in action. The Americans were also in a position to take charge of the increasing number of surrendering Germans. For their part the Poles were able to support the Americans with the 17 pounder guns of the 24th *Uhlans'* Fireflys and artillery observers who could call in supporting fires.

On 20 August 1944 the Polish position on the *Maczuga* lay on an elongated, wooded ridge running roughly north–south above the village of Coudehard. From their position on 262N the Poles had spectacular views to the west over the Dives River valley through which the Germans were endeavouring to escape. The western slopes of the ridge were steep which would hinder any attack from that direction. However the eastern part of the ridge was more open and in places overlooked from other hills which lay outside the Polish position. One route from Chambois, the D16 crossed the ridge to the south heading for Vimoutiers. This route was joined by the D242 which wound its way onto the ridge from la Cour du Bosq. Another route branched off from the D16 through a pass between 262N and 262S just south of the village of Mont Ormel, from which the ridge takes its name and heads towards Vimoutiers and the River Seine.

Although the terrain on the eastern portion of the *Maczuga* was fairly open, the rest of the position was covered with woods, *bocage* and undulating terrain. Tanks moved into defensive positions concealed in the edges of woods or in the hedges running alongside the fields and tracks. Infantry were dug in, interspersed between the tank and anti-tank gun positions. The general dispositions of the battlegroup on the *Maczuga* was as follows, divided between an "Eastern" and "Western" sector. In the east were the squadrons of the 2nd Armoured Regiment, interspersed with infantry from the 8th Battalion. In the west a company from 9th Infantry was deployed near the Boisjos Manor House. Because of its resemblance to a medieval fortification, it earned the nickname *Zameczka* (little castle). Astride the D242 were the *Podhale* Battalion and supporting armour. Further to the south of this position was the main body of the 9th Infantry Battalion. The 1st Armoured Regiment deployed its 1st and 2nd Squadrons covering the southern approaches to the position, with the 3rd covering the north, however these dispositions would change as the action developed.

The command and control arrangement for the coming engagement were unusual. The bulk of the 1st Polish Armoured Division's combat power was either deployed on the *Maczuga* or around Chambois. However neither of the division's two brigade headquarters had been deployed with them, despite the fact that both battlegroups were of brigade size. However these headquarters were probably best left behind, able to co-ordinate logistical and artillery support. In fact, the 10th Armoured Cavalry Brigade (Colonel Tadeusz Majewski) seems to have functioned as the higher-level headquarters, co-ordinating reports from the battlegroups on the *Maczuga* and in Chambois. However communication between the battlegroups and the rest of the division would be reliant on the wireless sets with the battalion headquarters and in the armoured regiments' tanks. Without the presence of an overall commander on the *Maczuga*, the senior officer was Lieutenant Colonel Zdzislaw Szydlowski, commanding officer of 9th Infantry Battalion but he had neither the time nor the communication resources to directly "command". So each of the various units looked after their particular sector, co-operating where necessary. That this was accomplished so successfully over the following days is a tribute, both to the training and professional skill of the various regimental and battalion commanders involved, and also to General Maczek's trust in the professional abilities of his men.

In the morning, as the mist lifted from the top of Mont Ormel the Poles could see dozens of columns moving across the Dives Valley to the west. During the course of the day the Polish defences would be assaulted by both organised and impromptu attacks from some of those groups trying to escape the pocket, together with more organised attacks from outside the encirclement, as German forces tried desperately to open up an escape corridor for their trapped comrades.

To do this II *SS-Panzerkorps* (9.*SS-Panzerdivision Hohenstaufen* and 2.*SS-Panzerdivision Das Reich*) with some 20 tanks, under the command of *Obergruppenfuhrer* Bittrich was ordered to break through the encirclement from outside. Their assault began at approximately 10.00, with attacks on 8th Battalion by two battalions from SS-*Panzergrenadierregiment 4*. This attack was between off, but was followed almost immediately by an attack on the northern end of the Western flank of the *Maczuga* by paratroopers from 3. *Fallschirmjaegerdivision*, supported by three assault guns, which were destroyed by 3rd Squadron 1st Armoured Regiment. Although these attacks were fought off, the restricted area of the *Maczuga* was constantly under fire from German mortars, artillery and *nebelwerfers* (multi-barrelled rocket launchers) which resulted in a steady stream of casualties. Prisoners were taken in ever increasing numbers and a temporary PoW cage was established in a small clearing in the woods named by the Poles as the *Polona* (glade) in the area held by 2nd Armoured Regiment and 8th Infantry Battalion. By the afternoon of 20 August some 800 PoWs were under guard. As all areas of the *Maczuga* were exposed to German indirect and direct fire, they also suffered casualties.

As the fighting continued, casualties mounted. Second Lieutenant Markiewicz one of the Division's Medical Officers (MO) established an Advanced Dressing Station (ADS), treating both Polish and German wounded in the *Zameczka* at Boisjos, to the north of the main Mace position. He was assisted by the 2nd Armoured Regiment's MO Lieutenant Władysław Kulesza and the 8th Infantry Battalion's MO, Second Lieutenant Wierdak who worked together carrying out amputations and blood transfusions, aided by chaplains Father Hupa and Father Rembowski. The *Zameczka* was constantly exposed to fire, despite the Red-Cross flags displayed. Such were the increasing number of casualties that not all could be accommodated in the *Zameczka*. Another ADS was set up down the hill in a nearby orchard with Second Lieutenant Drozdowski's Field Ambulance unit assisted by Second Lieutenant Szygowski, the 9th Infantry Battalion's MO. During the entire action on the

Maczuga, despite the often bitter and brutal nature of the fighting, Polish and German medical personnel worked together, treating the steadily increasing numbers of wounded, from both sides.

The eastern flank continued to be the most vulnerable area of the *Maczuga* for the German assaults. At 14.00 a German battalion-strength attack was mounted supported by PzKw IV tanks. Two were destroyed by 2nd Armoured Regiment tanks and anti-tank fire, with the Poles losing two tanks. At 15.00 the enemy launched another attack from the east, over the area of open ground between the D16 and D242. This, the most determined and sustained German assault of the day, was again made by infantry supported by PzKw IVs. It struck the boundary between the 8th and 9th Infantry battalions. The German intention was to split the Polish defence line and then overrun their entire defensive position. The attacks enjoyed some initial success and forced the Poles back towards Hill 262N. At the same time 3. *Fallschirmjaegerdivision* made another assault from inside the pocket. These combined attacks allowed the Germans to open up temporary escape routes north and south of the ridge along the D242 and D16. The survivors of 3. *Fallschirmjaegerdivision,* some 5000 men led by *General* Eugen Meindl commander of 2. *Fallschirmjaegerkorps* were able to make their escape. Also able to do so was the wounded 7. *Armee* Commander *Oberstgruppenfuhrer* Hausser.

Over and around the *Maczuga*, battle raged. The strength and violence of the German attack carried them deep into the Polish positions with desperate hand-to-hand fighting. After shooting off all their ammunition, the men of 9th Infantry Battalion's mortar platoon joined the fight as infantry. Polish tanks and German panzers engaged each other at point blank range, barrel-to barrel. By 17.00 the fighting was at its most intense, with the commander of the 2nd Armoured Regiment, Lieutenant Colonel Stanislaw Koszutski at its centre. As he was conferring with one of his officers he noticed a tank with "a diamond shaped turret and black cross" a few yards in front of his tanks and could hear others approaching. They were German! Koszutski ordered his tanks to open fire. At the same time the Germans launched a determined assault from the rear intending to overrun the Polish tanks. As the tanks engaged targets to their front with their guns, their crews had to fire hull and turret machine guns at the enemy infantry attacking from the rear, attempting to swamp the Poles. Tank commanders joined the defence, firing their pistols at Germans trying to clamber aboard their vehicles. Koszutski later described:.

> An incredible situation. All of the Regiment's machine guns are firing at the same time, all of the turret machine guns and all of the anti-aircraft machine guns in both directions – 44 tank guns and around 90 machine guns. The drone of German *Schmeissers* can clearly be heard among the explosions. The nervous tension is incredible. One can feel it running like an electric current across all units. It cannot last for long. It is the culminating point of the battle, the war, life, of something fundamental. Something has got to give. There is no leader in overall command, each one is fighting with weapon in hand.

By 19.00 hours the attack was finally driven off and the original Polish positions re-established. Both sides were exhausted, fighting was broken off for the night.

Earlier in the day, at the town of Saint Lambert, which the Canadians had captured the day before, the Germans had launched a final breakout attempt as waves of infantry supported by tanks assaulted the Canadian positions. By late afternoon some of the German survivors had escaped to the north-east and by the evening some of these group were endeavouring to make their way post the Polish positions in Chambois and on the *Maczuga*. These often *ad hoc* collections of troops from a variety of units took advantage of the fighting and mutual exhaustion of both attackers and defenders to infiltrate out of the pocket, with varying degrees of success. A *Waffen-SS* officer observed:

> Broken up into small groups of five or six men each, they advanced from hedge to hedge and through them, constantly covering and observing, mostly moving stealthily, sometimes leaping and running. On the pastures and in the ditches lay dead men, caught by enemy fire. They saw groups of soldiers who had thrown away their weapons and were waving white rags attached to sticks, indicating their willingness to surrender. A disgraceful, never before seen picture.

However, when the situation on the *Maczuga* permitted, Polish tanks would engage such groups of troops and vehicles with both their main armament and on-board machine guns inflicting further casualties on the retreating columns.

At Chambois, in the early morning the Germans attempted a mass breakout past the Polish and American positions. From its commanding position on Hill 113 the Cromwells of 10th Mounted Rifles, supported by some anti-tank guns opened a devastating fire on the retreating columns destroying tanks and other vehicles and inflicting heavy casualties on the fleeing enemy and receiving the surrender of many others. During this heavy fighting Major Jan Maciejowski, commanding officer of the Regiment was killed by a sniper (Major Otten Ejsymont assumed temporary command until Colonel Franciszek Skibinski was appointed on 22 August). Among the enemy captured was *Generalleutnant* Otto Elfeldt, officer commanding LXXXIV *Armeekorps,* the most senior German officer taken prisoner in the Falaise pocket, he was taken to Captain Michael Gutowski of the 10th Mounted Rifles, who offered the general his last cigarette. They conversed in French. Later, as German attacks continued, Elfeldt remarked that perhaps their positions as prisoner and captor might be reversed by the fortunes of war. "I do not surrender to Germans" was Gutowski's response.

Ammunition expenditures had been heavy, the 10th Mounted Rifles' 3rd Squadron had expended all its 75mm shells, and its last belts of ammunition for their on-board machine guns. The Regiment was ordered to abandon Hill 113 and fall back to the eastern side of Chambois. Enemy attacks ceased about 20.30.

Efforts had been made by divisional headquarters to get supplies of food, fuel and ammunition to both Chambois and the *Maczuga*. A supply convoy of three-ton trucks had been despatched on the 18 August, but the problems of navigating and moving along poor and narrow roads running through hills and valleys, and suffering casualties in encounters with enemy forces meant that it was not until 21 August that any major re-supply was possible.

In another effort to relieve the supply situation Lieutenant Jerzy Niewinowski, commander of the 2nd Armoured Regiment's reconnaissance section with three of his Stuart Mk V light tanks, fought his way off the *Maczuga* in an effort to make contact with the relieving 4th Canadian Armoured Division. His mission was successful and was able to return to the position with much needed fuel and ammunition. As a recognition for this act of bravery Lieutenant Niewinowski was awarded the *Virtuti Militari* Class V – Silver Cross for this exploit.

Although the Poles had been under intense pressure during the day they were able to call upon both artillery and air support.

There were at least five Forward Observation Officers (FOO), with the Polish forces on the *Maczuga* and in Chambois who could call on the impressive artillery resources at the Allies' disposal. On the *Maczuga* were two FOOs from the 1st Motorised Artillery Regiment and three from the 2nd Motorised Artillery Regiment. These observers could direct the fire of the 1st Polish Armoured Division's 25 pounder field guns. Additionally, there was also a FOO, Captain Pierre Sevigny from the 4th Medium Regiment, Royal Canadian Artillery equipped with more powerful 5.5 inch medium guns. As many of the officers and men of the division were more fluent in French, rather than English, having a French Canadian artillery observer made for easier and more speedy communication.

These observers were therefore able to direct heavy and regular concentrations of fire on the enemy. A FOO could call in a "MIKE" target where all of a regiment's guns could be directed onto a single target, a "UNCLE" target calling on all the division's guns and a "VICTOR" target which could call on a corps worth of artillery. During the action Captain Sevigny identified many MIKE and UNCLE targets and even a VICTOR. Such was the enemy pressure on the *Maczuga* that sometimes the FOOs had to take up rifles or man machine guns to join in the defence of the position. Ammunition expenditures were huge. On one day 2nd Motorised Artillery Regiment fired about 7,000 shells. This Regiment was firing at maximum range and moved its guns nearer the *Maczuga*. In doing so it encountered retreating Germans and engaged them over open sights.

Allied air strikes were not allowed on targets in the pocket itself but were directed on to the approaches of the narrowing exit. Although the 3-inch rockets carried by RAF Typhoon fighter-bombers were not particularly accurate, or effective, against tanks, used on infantry or transport their effects could be devastating. Other fighter-bombers dropped bombs or strafed targets with cannon or machine guns.

To the north, and outside the perimeter of the Polish position was Hill 239 which was occupied by the Germans. From this position at 0700 hours on 21 August German infantry supported by three Panther tanks attacked southwards towards Boisjos. Despite the Red-Cross flags the Polish medical ambulance unit came under fire. Father Hupa, the Padre of 9th Infantry Battalion, and some wounded were killed in an ambulance. Polish tanks were able to knockout or drive off the Panthers and the infantry withdrew, but the Poles continued to be the targets of German artillery and mortars.

At 11.00 an attack by *Waffen-SS* troops was made in the south, up the steeps slopes of the ridge near Coudehard. This almost suicidal attack was stopped by 20mm fire from Crusader anti-aircraft tanks. This was the last of the German assaults. The Poles, after several days of intense combat with little rest, were seriously short of ammunition, fuel and rations.

However, the end of their ordeal was at hand. At noon the 4th Canadian Armoured Brigade broke through to the *Maczuga*. Its war diary recorded:

> The picture at Hill 262 was the grimmest the regiment has so far come up against. The Poles had no supplies for three days; they had several hundred wounded who had not been evacuated, about 700 prisoners of war lay loosely guarded in a field, the road was blocked with burnt out vehicles, both our own and the enemy. Unburied dead and parts of them were strewn about by the score...The Poles cried with joy when we arrived and from what they said I doubt if they will ever forget this day and the help we gave them.

In Chambois the British 50th Infantry Division relieved the Poles and Americans.

At the same time German commanders recorded that the arrival of their troops from the encirclement had ceased. With the closing of the Falaise Gap the Battle of Normandy came to an end.

Victory did not come cheap. The fighting around the *Maczuga* cost the Poles some 351 killed, approximately 1,000 wounded, 114 missing and 10 tanks lost. In total the 1st Polish Armoured Division suffered 1,441 casualties during the Normandy campaign with 325 killed, 1,002 wounded, 114 missing (including 60 officers). Casualties for the entire campaign in North-West Europe 1944-45 would reach 5,098 (1,294 killed).

German losses have been estimated as 2,000 killed, 5,000 taken prisoner. Left on the battlefield were 55 tanks, of which six were Tigers, 14 Panthers, 44 guns and 152 armoured vehicles, 359 vehicles of all types were destroyed.

In assessing the battle to seal the Falaise Pocket as a whole, there is some dispute as to the number of casualties the Germans sustained (estimates vary between 80,000 – 100,000 encircled; 10-15,000 killed, 40-50,000 PoW). Inside the pocket US Army investigators counted 5,000 trucks, 380 tanks and 160 self-propelled guns destroyed or abandoned. The British, Canadians and Poles counted a further 344 armoured vehicles in their sectors.

However, the Germans were able to extricate some 165,000 men from the Falaise pocket and over the River Seine, the next major barrier across their line of retreat.

Nevertheless, the effects of the victory in which the 1st Polish Armoured Division had played such a prominent role were far reaching. When the German commanders began the retreat from Normandy their hope had been to establish a new line of defence along the Seine. The combat actions of the 1st Polish Armoured Division between 19-21 August 1944 were instrumental in thwarting this plan. Those forces that did escape were too disorganised and demoralised and, together with the heavy losses of equipment, had no alternative but to fall back, almost to the very borders of the *Reich*. Paris was liberated on 25 August. The Allies conducted a vigorous pursuit of the retreating Germans, fanning out across France and into Belgium.

General Montgomery rightly described the Poles at Falaise as 'the cork in the bottle" in his tribute. The combat actions of the 1st Polish Armoured Division on the *Maczuga* and at Chambois, truly memorialised by the relieving Canadians as "a Polish Battlefield", remain one of the most effective examples of the conduct of operations by combined arms formations by any of the Western Allies during World War II. That this achievement was possible is a testament to the skill, bravery, dedication and determination of its officers and men and of the highest qualities of command and leadership of their leader, *General Brygady* Stanislaw Maczek.

The *Maczuga*

161. Firefly, Mace , Normandy, 19-21 August 1944. A Sherman Firefly concealed amongst trees and bushes on the western flank of the *Maczuga* (Mace), Hill 262N, overlooking the Dives river valley. The shape of the contour lines of this feature on his maps reminded General Maczek of a medieval Polish weapon. Two of the Firefly's crew, both wearing tank crew helmets and Denim coveralls check the vehicle and its camouflage, consisting of recently cut foliage. The Fireflys from the 1st and 2nd Armoured Regiments deployed on the *Maczuga*, together with the towed 17 pounder anti-tank guns from the 1st Anti-Tank Regiment were the most powerful weapons available to its defenders, being able to take on the heaviest German tanks. Over the course of the battle the Polish tanks taking advantage of the cover provided by trees and hedges and could rapidly move from one threatened area of the *Maczuga* to another. One of the crewmen is carrying an Mk III Sten sub-machine gun. During the ferocious German attacks against the positions of 2nd Armoured Regiment at about 17.00 on 20 August, such weapons offered a last line of defence for the embattled crews.(PISM)

162. Bofors, Mace, Normandy, 19-21 August 1944. At least one battery (18 guns) from the divisional light anti-aircraft unit, the 1st Anti-Aircraft Regiment, was deployed on the 'Mace'. Together with the Crusader Mk II/III anti-aircraft tanks from the Armoured Regiments they would have been used to defend against any Luftwaffe attacks (however unlikely) against the Polish forces on the *Maczuga*. However, both were deployed with great effect on ground targets. Here Polish gunners prepare one of their 40mm Bofors mounted on a Morris C9/B lorries. A soldier on the right with binoculars appears to be scanning the sky, on the look-out for enemy aircraft. The gun has been heavily camouflaged to blend in with the local scenery and its barrel has been lowered to the horizontal, ready to engage ground targets. (*With the Tanks of the 1st Polish Armoured Division. K. Jamar. H.L.SMIT & ZN, Hengelo, 1946*)

163. Seventeen Pounder Anti-tank Gun, Mace, Normandy, 19-21 August 1944. A 17 pounder anti-tank gun from the 1st Anti-Tank Regiment camouflaged and ready to open fire. To dig a towed 17 pounder into a prepared defensive position could take up to 12-15 hours, but this seems a more hastily prepared firing position as the gun appears not to have been fully dug in. Unlike the tanks which could be moved quickly within the *Maczuga* position, the 17 pounders would have been relatively immobile as they were difficult to manhandle and needed to be towed into position. This gun and its crew are ready for action. The trails have been opened out and the spades dug-in to absorb the powerful recoil. The gun-layer is in position on the left-hand side of the gun and the loader to the left cradles an anti-tank round ready to push into the breach of the gun. Both the soldier behind the gun-layer appears to be carrying a Mk II Sten sub-machine gun and the soldier to the loader's right a Sten Mk III sub-machine, as their personal weapons. (*With the Tanks of the 1st Polish Armoured Division. K. Jamar.H.L.SMIT & ZN, Hengelo, 1946*)

164. The *Zameczka*, Boisjos Manor House, Mace, Normandy, 19-21 August 1944. The manor house at Boisjos, to the north of the main Mace position. Here Second Lieutenant Markiewicz one of the Division's Medical Officers (MO) established an Advanced Dressing Station (ADS), treating both Polish and German wounded. He was assisted by the 2nd Armoured Regiment's Medical Officer (MO) Lieutenant Doctor Władysław Kulesza (see photo 183) and the 8th Infantry Battalion's MO, Second Lieutenant Wierdak who worked together carrying out amputations and blood transfusions with the aid of chaplains Father Hupa and Father Rembowski. Because of its resemblance to a medieval fortification the Boisjos manor house was named the *Zameczka* (little castle). It was constantly exposed to fire, despite the Red-Cross flags. By the end of the end of the battle the *Zameczka* was attending to some 300 wounded (from both sides), many forced to lie in the open due to lack of room inside. It was not until the afternoon of 21st August before a long convoy of vehicles was able to evacuate the wounded. The white painted lorry is a Canadian Military Pattern (CMP) 3-ton truck serving as an ambulance, was probably part of that convoy. (PISM)

165. Panther, Mace, Normandy, 21 August 1944. A knocked-out PzKw V Panther. At 0700 hours on 21 August German infantry supported by three Panther tanks attacked southwards towards Boisjos. Despite the Red-Cross flags, the medical unit was fired upon and Father Hupa, Padre, 9th Infantry Battalion, and some wounded were killed. Polish tanks counter-attacked knocking out this Panther and driving off the others. (PISM)

166. Sherman Vs, Mace, Normandy, 19-21 August 1944. Two Sherman Vs concealed behind thick hedgerows and trees, the tanks themselves are camouflaged with foliage. This shows the defensive advantage afforded by such cover. This photo may have been taken after the repulse of one of the numerous German attacks. The casualties in the foreground are probably German. The near most figure appears to be wearing a belt with a metal buckle similar to that issued to the German Army and *Waffen-SS*. In the background the crew of another Sherman are working on their tank, seemingly showing little concern for the nearby bodies. (*2nd Polish Armoured Regiment in Action, From Caen to Wilhelmshaven. Tadeusz Wiatrowski, Schlutersche Buchdrucferei, Hanover, 1946*)

167. Polish Casualties, Mace, Normandy, 19-21 August 1944. Two "walking wounded" Polish soldiers are led from the forward combat zone. From their berets they are probably injured crewmen from a damaged or knocked-out tank. They have probably been treated at the Regimental Aid Post (RAP). The soldiers assisting, one of whom is wearing a red-cross armband, and who both wear the Royal Armoured Corps rimless helmet are probably from the RAP. The wounded men will probably evacuated by ambulance to the Advanced Dressing Station established at the *Zameczka* to the North of Hill 262N. Behind them is a Sherman V, also seen in photo 168 (with another parked behind). The commander is in his turret hatch. The Allied White-star recognition symbol is displayed between the two applique armour plates. Its turret is slightly rotated to the left with its gun barrel depressed. (PISM)

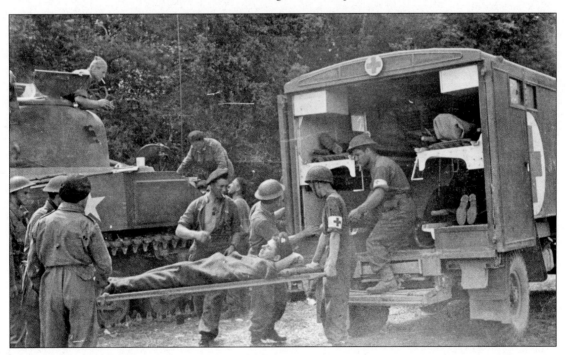

168. Polish Casualties and K2 Ambulance, Mace, Normandy, 19-21 August 1944. Casualties, who have received some medical attention at the RAP, are evacuated by ambulance to the Advanced Dressing Station, the next stage in the casualty evacuation process, where more sophisticated medical treatment facilities should be available. The ambulance is an Austin "Katie" ambulance, so nicknamed because of its British Army K2 designation. This was the standard ambulance of British and British equipped armies throughout the war. The three ton vehicle could accommodate ten casualties or four stretcher cases. The soldier on the stretcher may be from a tank crew as he is wearing a beret. Other soldiers, some wearing tank crew berets and overalls, some infantrymen in Mk II steel helmets help in the evacuation procedure. Behind them is a Sherman V, the same tank as in the previous image. (PISM)

169. **Advanced Dressing Station, Mace, Normandy, 19-21 August 1944**. Such were the increasing number of casualties that not all could be accommodated in the Boisjos *Zameczka*. Another Advanced Dressing Station(ADS) was set up down the hill in a nearby orchard with Second Lieutenant Drozdowski's Field Ambulance unit assisted by Second Lieutenant Szygowski, the 9th Infantry Battalion's MO. Here in the orchard Polish and German wounded are being treated. Judging by their boots, the wounded on the left are probably Polish, while those on the right appear to be German. The two standing medical orderlies (both wearing Red Cross armbands) are German, the one on the right wearing the German Army *Einheitsfeldmütze* (standard field cap). Behind the orderlies is a Sherman tank from "C" Squadron (identified by the circle symbol on the rear of the tank's hull) of the 2nd Armoured Regiment. (*2nd Polish Armoured Regiment in Action, From Caen to Wilhelmshaven. Tadeusz Wiatrowski, Schlutersche Buchdrucferei, Hanover, 1946*)

170. **Polish and German Medical Orderlies, Mace, Normandy, 19-21 August 1944**. Although the fighting on the Mace was characterised by close combat, often with no quarter given, medical teams from both sides worked together in an attempt to do all they could for the mounting number of casualties, both Polish and German. Here a Polish medical orderly, himself suffering from a head wound, stands with a number of German soldiers, the one on the left and in the truck are wearing Red Cross armbands. The vehicle is probably a box-body version of the Opel "*Blitz*" three-ton truck widely used by all branches of the *Wehrmacht* throughout World War II. This example is probably temporally serving as an ambulance. In the background is a German VW 166 *Schwimmwagen* an amphibious vehicle based on the Volkswagen chassis, which has probably been taken over by the Poles. (PISM)

171. Advanced Dressing Station, Mace, Normandy, 19-21 August 1944. Another view of the dressing station (see also photo 169). Although under the cover of trees, the wounded would be vulnerable to shell bursts from artillery or mortars. The medical orderly with the Red Cross armband appears to be German. In the distant background is a civilian car, perhaps one commandeered by the Germans and now captured by the Poles. Part of a vehicle can be seen at the extreme right of the picture, possibly a M5 half-track, perhaps serving as an armoured ambulance. (*2nd Polish Armoured Regiment in Action, From Caen to Wilhelmshaven. Tadeusz Wiatrowski, Schlutersche Buchdrucferei, Hanover, 1946*)

172. Burial Party, Mace, Normandy, 19-21 August 1944. A joint Polish and German burial party lower a dead soldier into a temporary grave, alongside three previous burials. The soldier to the left is wearing British uniform with the soldier on the right, wearing a Red Cross armband, a jacket, rather than battledress, and German Army *Marschstiefel* (marching boots) is therefore probably German. Over the period of the fighting in defence of the Mace the Poles took an increasing number of PoWs. Having no safe area in which to secure them they were kept under guard in the '*Polona*' (glade or clearing) slightly screened by a ridge. By the afternoon of 20 August some 800 PoWs were under guard. As all areas of the Mace were exposed to German indirect and direct fire, the PoWs also suffered casualties. The vehicle in the right background is a German amphibious VW 166 *Schwimmwagen* (probably the same vehicle as seen in photo 170). (*2nd Polish Armoured Regiment in Action, From Caen to Wilhelmshaven. Tadeusz Wiatrowski, Schlutersche Buchdrucferei, Hanover, 1946*)

173. Firefly and Jagdpanther, Mace, Normandy, 19-21 August 1944. Many of the tank versus tank engagements were often at point blank range as the Germans desperately attempted to overcome the Polish defenders of the Mace blocking their escape routes out of the Falaise Pocket. So closely pressed were the attacks that combat often took place barrel to barrel, as here. A knocked out Firefly stands only a few feet away from a knocked out *Jagdpanther* (Hunting Panther). Note the closed nature of the hilly and wooded terrain on the Mace which often resulted in engagements being fought at such close ranges. Based on the Panther chassis the 45.5 ton *Jagdpanther* was one of the most effective German armoured fighting vehicles deployed in Normandy mounting a very powerful, limited traverse 8.8 cm Pak 43. Only small numbers saw service in Normandy with 654 *Schwere Panzerjaeger-Abteilung* (Heavy Tank Destroyer Battalion). The Firefly, with its 17 pounder gun was the only Allied tank in Normandy that was able to take on the *Jagdpanther*. The front of an Opel *"Blitz"* three-ton truck can be seen on the left. (PISM)

174. Sherman, Mace, Normandy, 19-21 August 1944. A knocked-out Sherman V, possibly from the 2nd Armoured Regiment at the northern end of the Mace. This vehicle may have been a victim of the German attack from the north and north-east on the 8th Infantry battalion on the afternoon of 20th August. The assault was made in battalion strength and was supported by PzKw IVs. The attack was halted and Polish infantry took many prisoners. Two *panzers* were destroyed by 2nd Armoured Regiment Shermans and towed anti-tank guns. The 1st Squadron of the 2nd Armoured Regiment lost two tanks in the action and this Sherman may be one of them. (PISM)

175. Seventeen Pounder Anti-tank Gun, Mace, Normandy, 19-21 August 1944. A 17 pounder anti-tank gun from the 1st Anti-Tank Regiment. Along with the 17 pounder equipped Fireflys this was the most powerful anti-tank weapon available to the Poles defending the Mace. The opportunities for concealment provided by the hedges and woods on the position can be seen here. This gun is probably in process of being relocated, as the trails have been secured together for towing. At 4,600 lbs, the 17 pounder was difficult to manhandle, so it will probably be moved to its new location by vehicle and is now ready to be attached to its tow, either a Quad or M5 half-track. (PISM)

176. Panther, Mace, Normandy, 19-21 August 1944. A knocked-out PzKw V Panther ausf A. The Panther was the second most numerous German tank faced by the Allies in Normandy (some 650 saw action during the campaign) and it was issued to nearly all of the German Panzer Divisions deployed. A 50-ton medium tank with a powerful 75mm KwK (*KampfwagenKanone*) 42 gun and very effective sloped armour it was a formidable enemy and could only be effectively countered by the Firefly with its 17 pounder gun. This vehicle has been pushed off the road to clear the way for allied traffic. (PISM)

177. German Casualties, Mace area, Normandy, 19-21 August 1944. Two dead German Infantrymen surrounded by the remains of their equipment lie in a field. They are probably the victims of an artillery bombardment. An open ammunition box lies between the two bodies. Alongside the soldier in the centre is his *Karabiner 98k*, the standard German infantry rifle throughout the war. He wears *Marschstiefel* (marching boots), by this stage of the war most German infantry wore shorter ankle-boots to economise on the limited supplies of leather. (PISM)

178. Panther, Mace, Normandy, 19-21 August 1944. A knocked-out Panther, unit unidentified, numbered 314, 3rd Company, 1st Platoon, 4TH vehicle (PISM)

179. Calvary, Mace, Normandy, 19-21 August 1944. The Calvary on the D16 at the southern end of the Mace, showing the ferocity of the fighting. In the left foreground is a destroyed German staff car that may be a commandeered French Citroen *Traction Avant* (front-wheel drive) saloon. A restored Calvary stands in the same place today as a memorial. (PISM)

180. Jagdpanzer IV, Mace, Normandy, 19-21 August 1944. A further illustration of the bitter fighting around the Mace, this photo was taken around the Mont Ormel First World War memorial, seen on the right, at a crossroads, a short distance from the D16. The knocked out vehicle is a *Jagdpanzer* IV, a self-propelled tank-destroyer based on a PzKw IV chassis and mounting a 75mm Pak 39L/48 gun. It was deployed in the *Panzerjaegerabteilung* (Anti-tank battalion) of a number of German *Panzer* Divisions in Normandy. 1st Polish Armored Division encountered this vehicle type during fighting with *SS-Panzerjaegerabteilung 12* from *12.SS-Panzerdivision* during Operations TOTALIZE and TRACTABLE. (PISM)

181. German Casualties, Mace area, Normandy, 19-21 August 1944. Two more German casualties. The foreground soldier is an infantryman. Behind his right shoulder is the characteristic German cylindrical metal gas-mask container, to its right is a water bottle. His *Karabiner 98K* rifle lies beside him. He and his comrade were probably victims of an artillery bombardment. (PISM)

182. Mace veterans, 2nd Armoured Regiment, Beveren-Waas, Belgium, 2 March 1946. Presentation of the town's coat of arms along with a colour, following the town's gratitude following liberation. Lieutenant Jerzy Niewinowski (left) commander of the 2nd Armoured Regiment's reconnaissance section with three of his Stuart tanks, fought his way off the Mace to make contact with the relieving Canadians, was awarded the Virtuti Militari class V- Silver Cross for this heroism. Another veteran of the Mace was standard bearer Sergeant-Major Alexsander Leon Jarzembowski. (AHA)

183. Mace veterans, 2nd Armoured Regiment, Lieutenant Dr. Władysław Kulesza (left) and Lieutenant Janusz Barbarski, 2nd Armoured Regiment. This photograph was taken later in the war. Barbarski's tank named 'Kitus II', behind the two officers, is a Sherman MkIIA issued to the 1st Polish Armoured Division a few months after the Normandy Campaign. (AHA)

Chambois

184. Chambois, Normandy, 19 August 1944. The Falaise Pocket is finally blocked! In Chambois troops from the Polish and US Armies linked up to complete the encirclement of the trapped German armies. This link-up is symbolised as John Wellington (left) of the US 359th Infantry Regiment shakes hands with Corporal Grabowski (right) of the 10th Dragoons (note battlefield trophies worn, German binoculars and Luger pistol holster). Private Wellington has an US Army M1 Carbine slung over his shoulder. The 359th Infantry Regiment was part of the US Army's 90th Infantry Division, carrying over its nickname "Tough 'Ombres" from its Great War predecessor. (PISM)

185. Sherman and PzKw IV H, Chambois, Normandy, 19-21 August 1944. Polish and American troops inspect destroyed German equipment in Chambois. Polish troops from a battle group formed from the 24th *Uhlans* Armoured Regiment and infantry from the 10th Dragoons Regiment attacked the town from the north-east and entered the town in the early afternoon of 19 August. The soldier on the immediate left is probably from the US 90th Infantry Division that made the first contact with the Poles at about 1900 hours, when Lieutenant Jan Karcz, a platoon commander from the 10th Polish Dragoons, made contact with Captain L.E Waters a company commander from the 359th Infantry Regiment. The tank is a Sherman probably from the 24th *Uhlans*. The German vehicle to its right is a knocked-out PzKw IV H medium tank. (PISM)

186. PzKw IV H Chambois, Normandy, 19-21 August 1944. A Polish Soldier looks inside the turret of a knocked-out PzKw IV H (the same vehicle as in the previous image 185) in Chambois. Judging by the melted remains of its road-wheel tires the vehicle caught fire, either when attacked or after being destroyed by its crew. The 26-ton PzKw IV H entered service in 1943. Round the turret is a screen of protective "schurzen" armour. Although Polish Shermans and Cromwells could be knocked out by the PzKw IV H, with its 75mm Kwk 40 gun, it was equally vulnerable to their 75mm guns. The PzKw IV was similar in size and silhouette to the Tiger heavy tank and the frequently reported sightings of Tigers by Allied tank crews were usually mistaken identifications of the much less formidable PzKw IV. (PISM)

187. Chambois, Normandy, 19 August 1944. Polish and American officers confer in Chambois. The American Captain, two bar rank badge on the front of his helmet, leans on the open hood of a US army jeep. The GI to his left has a slung M1 Garand rifle. The Polish infantry lieutenant, probably from the 10th Dragoons carries his field dressing tucked under the camouflage scrim of his Mark II steel helmet. After elements from the 1st Polish Armoured Division and the US 90th Infantry Division made contact during the late afternoon on 19 August, the officers of both units jointly organised the defence of the town. The Americans took responsibility for the southern portion of the town. The Poles for the north side. (PISM)

188. Chambois, Normandy, 20 August 1944. The temporary burial place for Major Jan Maciejowski (1904-44), commanding officer, 10th Mounted Rifle Regiment ((*10 Pulk Strzelow Konnych*), killed by a sniper on 20 August at Chambois. His Royal Armoured Corps helmet surmounts the wooden cross. In 1925 he was commissioned as a second lieutenant in the 27th *Uhlan* Regiment. He remained a cavalryman and by 1939 was a squadron commander. In France he became Commanding Officer of 2nd Squadron, 10th Mounted Rifles Regiment and from 4 June 1940 its second-in-command. After escaping to Great Britain, he commanded the Regiment's heavy machine guns. From March 1942 onwards he was once again the Regiment's second-in-command. In November 1943, now a Major, he became Commanding Officer of the 10th Mounted Rifles, the divisional armoured reconnaissance regiment. He was wounded at Jort on 14 August when his Cromwell tank ran over a mine. He was killed a few days later. He was posthumously promoted to the rank of Colonel on 25 November 1944. The cross is marked with the following dedication (PISM):

Ian Maciejowski

Major Polish Army

Commander of the 10th Regiment Cavalry Rifles

Died on the field of glory

20.08.1944 at 1 o clock at Chambois

189. Chambois, Normandy, 19-21 August 1944. A German VW type 166 *Schwimmwagen* amphibious vehicle with at least four wounded passengers, including a stretcher case. The figure on the right of the vehicle, who may be wearing the red-cross marked white surcoat sometimes worn by German medical personnel, appears to be unwounded. They may have been captured with the vehicle or a captured vehicle is being used as a temporary ambulance. These vehicles were widely used by reconnaissance and engineering units and for liaison, particularly where an amphibious capability might be useful. (PISM)

190. Chambois, Normandy, August, 1944. A Polish soldier (right) and two American soldiers (left) explore a local road and inspect abandoned and destroyed German vehicles. (PISM)

After the Battle

191. Captured *Kubelwagen*, Normandy, August 1944. A fairly intact *Kubelwagen* taken into service by the 10th Mounted Rifles who have indicated its change of ownership by the large inscription on the side and by the addition of an allied white star recognition symbol. Such "war trophies" were popular, but the provision of spare parts for captured vehicle often proved problematical. There were also dangers in using captured equipment. Distinctive sound or silhouette might prompt one's own side to "shoot first and ask questions later"! Hence, in this case, the white star and wording, note the smaller 'Poland' just visible on the left side door panel. In the background stand two Bedford trucks. (*1st Polish Armoured Division (1 VIII 1944 – 11 XI 1944) France-Belgium-Holland. Breda-Osterhout*)

192. Normandy, August 1944. A knocked-out German *Flakpanzer* (anti-aircraft tank) 38t. Issued to the anti-aircraft platoon of *panzer* regiments, using the body of the Pz 38t tank produced in Czechoslovakia. The superstructure was modified to take a single 2 cm Flak 38 light anti-aircraft gun. Side plates could be folded-down (as here) to allow the gun to be traversed through 360 degrees. By 1944 this was inadequate to deal with the Allied air threat encountered in Normandy. Further up the road is a destroyed Sd.Kfz. 250 light armoured half-track. In the rear is a destroyed/abandoned *Panzerjager* (tank hunter) 38(t) *Marder* III. (PISM)

193. Normandy, August, 1944. Polish soldiers examine an abandoned PzKw II light tank. This was a "Blitzkrieg" era German tank armed with a 20mm automatic cannon. Developed pre-war it was the primary German tank in service during the invasion of Poland in 1939 and France in 1940 , but obsolete in 1944. This example has either been retained for training or used for internal security purposes. Behind it is a Sd.Kfz 7/2 half-track mounting a 3.7 Flak 37. This version has been fitted with an armoured cab and can be seen just behind the PzKw II. (PISM)

194. Chambois, Normandy, 19-21 August 1944. Dead horses and smashed carts litter one of the escape routes out of the Falaise Pocket. The German Army, particularly its infantry divisions were heavily dependent on draft horses to move its supply wagons and artillery pieces. Thousands of horses became casualties during the German retreat. Further down the road there is an abandoned Panther tank while immediately behind it a PzKw IV. By them is a destroyed German staff car. (PISM)

195. Normandy, 19 August 1944. Abandoned and smashed *Panje* (Magyar for "pony") wagons. Used by Eastern European peasant farmers, their high wheels and boat shaped body made them ideal to negotiate mud and snow. As these wagons were usually the only way to move supplies through the harsh conditions of the Eastern Front they were commandeered in large numbers. German forces also made extensive use of these wagons in the west, as units, transferred from one front to another, brought these carts with them. (PISM)

196. Normandy, August, 1944. As well as hundreds of destroyed items of military equipment, there were thousands of bodies to recover and bury. Here German dead have been collected and loaded on to a trailer towed by a medical jeep (fitted with a top rail for carrying stretchers). The Arm of Service number "57" indicates the junior battalion in the senior brigade in an infantry division. The trailer appears to be an airborne jeep trailer that the unit may have "acquired" and possibly repainted. The formation sign on the bottom left hand corner does have a resemblance to the Polar Bear flash of the 49 (West Riding) Division. If this is the case, the unit concerned is the Hallamshire Battalion, Yorkshire and Lancashire Regiment and the jeep would be from one of the division's attached RAMC units, either 146 Field Ambulance, 160 Field Ambulance, 187 Field Ambulance or possibly 16 or 17 Field Dressing Stations who may have borrowed the trailer for this less than pleasant duty. (PISM)

197. Normandy, August 1944. Three Polish soldiers stand proudly before a knocked out PzKw V Panther, which appears to have lost its right-hand track. Most Panthers encountered in Normandy were of the second production variant, the a*usfuhuring* (version) A. However this is a much rarer (for Normandy) Panther a*usfuhuring* G which incorporated a number of changes to the original design resulting from operational experience. Armour protection was improved and, ammunition storage capacity increased. The most visible difference between the two varients was the distinctive side sloped mudguard shape, of the *ausfuhuring* G seen here. The original German crew of this vehicle have hung spare track links to the side of the turret as additional protection, in a similar manner to their allied adversaries. (PISM)

198. Normandy, August 1944. A knocked-out German PzKw IV H. One of its road wheels has been damaged and the barrel of its 75mm KwK 40 is depressed. It has protective *shurzen* additional armour mounted around its turret. (PISM)

199. Normandy, 19 August 1944. Destroyed German vehicles block a narrow road. The vehicle in the foreground is a Citroen type 11 UB Ambulance. Originally built for the French Army before the war, many were taken into German service. This example does not appear to be carrying any Red-Cross markings. Behind it, further down the road is a German Sd.kfz 10 half-track. (PISM)

200. Normandy, August, 1944. Polish soldiers examine two PzKw IV H in the corner of a Normandy field. Because of the elevation of their gun barrels the two tanks do not appear to have been in action and so may have been abandoned by their crews. The more distant tank has *schurzen* around its turret. The PzKw IV H on the left still carries a number of its *schurzen* side plates, although one is missing. The turret hatch is open and part of the *schurzen* has been folded back to allow access. (PISM)

201. Normandy, August 1944. Abandoned German half-tracks. In the front, left is a Sd.Kfz. 251 aus D, the standard armoured carrier for the *panzer grenadiers* in German *Panze*r divisions. Usually one of the four panzer grenadier battalions in a *Heer panzer* division, and one in six in their *Waffen-SS* equivalents were so equipped. This vehicle carries the *1. SS-Panzerdivision Leibstandarte Adolf Hitler* divisional insignia on the left of its front plate. To its right is the German tactical sign indicating that it used to be part of the *III Bataillon, SS-Panzergrenadierregiment 2*. Behind it, a soldier is examining the interior of a German Army Sd.Kfz 250 (it carries a WH registration marking). This was a light half-tracked vehicle used for a wide variety of roles throughout the war. To increase production, the design was simplified and given the designation "*Neu*" (new) and is the type shown here. (PISM)

202. Normandy, August 1944. A Polish soldier moves through a group of destroyed German trucks. The soldier is carrying a Sten Mk III sub-machine gun. The remains of an Opel "Blitz" lorry, the German Army's standard 3-ton truck, are to his left. Immediately to its rear are the remains of a Renault AHN medium truck. During the occupation, some 4,000 were manufactured for the German Army at the Renault Billancourt factory. Another Renault AHN can be seen up against the trees to the rear. (PISM)

203. Normandy, August, 1944. A blocked road in the area around Mont Ormel. The road is full of abandoned vehicles and discarded pieces of uniform and equipment. The vehicles appear relatively undamaged and have probably been abandoned by their crews attempting to escape by foot, thus leaving this narrow road blocked. Two soldiers are standing behind an unidentified lorry laden with supplies. The "WL" vehicle registration plate on the rear of the truck on the right, up against the hedge identifies it as a *Luftwaffe* vehicle. The very large vehicle in the background may be a Sd.Kfz 9 half-track tractor. On its rear it is carrying a foliage camouflaged BMW R75 motor bike and side car combination and on the road behind it is a motorbike. Soldiers attempting to escape the encirclement were at an advantage if they were in tracked or half-track vehicles that could move across country, but many, when faced by such congestion just sat and waited for an opportunity to surrender to the advancing allies. (PISM)

204. Normandy, August, 1944. A different view of the vehicles in photo 203 taken from in front of the Sd.kfz 9 half-track which its registration numbers show to be a *Luftwaffe* vehicle. It may be from the III *Flakkorps* which deployed many of its 8.8 cm Flak guns in both the anti-aircraft and anti-tank role. The overturned truck in front may be part of the same unit and a large quantity of the ammunition boxes it was carrying, has spilled across the road. (PISM)

205. Normandy, August, 1944. A higher angle view of the vehicles seen in photos 203 and 204. The overturned truck in front of the Sd.Kfz 9 is a French Renault AHN medium truck. In the immediate foreground are the remains of a 2 cm Flak 38 light anti-aircraft gun. To its right is a very badly damaged motor bike. Polish soldiers sift through the wreckage. (PISM)

206. Normandy, August 1944. A destroyed VW 82 *Kubelwagen* blocks a narrow road. A dead German soldier is to the left and an abandoned German steel helmet lies on the road in the foreground. The German equivalent of the Jeep, the *Kubelwagen* was designed by Dr. Ferdinand Porsche as a light military utility vehicle and as such, large numbers served in all branches of the *Wehrmacht* throughout the war (and beyond). Behind it is the rear of an Sd.Kfz 10 half-track. (PISM)

207. Normandy, August 1944. The view from alongside the Sd.Kfz 10 half-track seen in the previous image. More destroyed vehicles and in front of them, a 2cm Flak 38 still on its Sd. Ah. 52 trailer. (PISM)

208. Normandy, August, 1944. In the distance can be seen an overturned 10.5 cm leFH 18 field gun. To the left of the central vehicle can be seen another truck which has overturned blocking the road. A dead German soldier lies on the road in the foreground and the wreckage of an unidentified vehicle is at the extreme left of the picture. (PISM)

209. Normandy, August, 1944. The same scene as in the previous image. However, in the distance a soldier stands by the overturned field gun.

210. Normandy, August, 1944. A close-up view of the left side of the scene shown in the previous image. The large vehicle to the right carries a "WL" registration number. Dead German soldiers lie along the side of the road. (PISM)

211. Normandy, August 1944. A Polish soldier inspects the overturned 10.5 cm leFH 18 (*leichte FeldHaubitze* "light field howitzer") the standard medium divisional German artillery piece throughout the war. The Sd.kfz 9 towing vehicle is a Luftwaffe vehicle so perhaps this is a gun from one of the artillery regiments from 3. *Fallschirmjaegerdivision* which was one of the units trapped in the encirclement.

212. Normandy, August 1944. Three German trucks block a Normandy road. (PISM)

213. Normandy, August 1944. A closer view of the vehicles in the preceding image. The two trucks in the foreground and possibly the third obscured to their rear are Ford V3000 trucks. The 3-ton Ford V3000 was the second most produced German military truck after the Opel *Blitz*. Both of the front vehicles appear to have been abandoned with the doors on both open. The trucks have been partly camouflaged with foliage. The one on the right is a box-body version and may be serving as a workshop or possibly office vehicle. The lorry to the left seems to be the standard truck version. Intriguingly a chair lies on the ground to the front of this vehicle. (PISM)

214. Normandy, August, 1944. A Polish soldier from an armoured regiment (he wears the RAC rimless tank crewman's helmet) examines items he has found in and around a destroyed German staff car, probably a commandeered French Citroen *Traction Avant* saloon. (PISM)

215. Normandy, August, 1944. A badly damaged Horch Kfz 17 radio truck with the body of one of its former occupants lying alongside. The medium off-road passenger car built by Opel and Auto Union saw wide service with the German armed forces during the war, in a variety of roles. The Kfz 17 was a variant used by signal units. (PISM)

216. Normandy, August, 1944. A wrecked German workshop lorry, surrounded by debris. Behind it is a Fiat *Topolino* (little mouse). In 1935 the Italian Fiat company began work on a small car for low income families. At the start of World War II many of these cars were pressed into military service. Most were used as run-about's by the Italian and German armies, seeing service in Europe, North Africa, the Soviet Union and here in France. (PISM)

217. Normandy, August 1944. An abandoned PzKw IV H. A human leg can be seen atop the turret. *Shurzen* protective armour surrounds the turret. The turret number "562" indicates the tank was the second vehicle in the sixth platoon of number five company. A German Panzer Regiment was organised into two *Abteilung* (battalion) each of four companies consecutively numbered 1-8. Therefore this vehicle is from the second *Abteilung* of a *panzer* division. The uneven surface on the side of the hull below the turret is the result of the application of *Zimmerit*. The Germans developed hand-held shaped charges fitted with powerful magnets that an infantryman could attach to an enemy tank. In 1943, the Germans, concerned that their enemies might develop a similar weapon, began applying a putty-like anti-magnetic paste, developed by Zimmer AG, to the vulnerable surfaces of their armoured vehicles. The practice was ended in September 1944 when the Germans became concerned that the anti-magnetic paste might be a fire hazard, and also because none of their enemies had developed the type of anti-tank weapon that *Zimmerit* was supposed to defeat. (PISM)

218. Normandy, August, 1944. A hastily dug grave of a German *Fallschirmjaeger* (Paratrooper). The helmet on the grave is the distinctive parachute helmet issued to the *Fallschirmjaeger*. It was probably dug as a temporary grave by the soldier's comrades, probably members of the 3. *Fallschirmjaegerdivision*. On 20th August this division unsuccessfully attacked the northern end of the Western flank of the Mace in an effort to breakout of the encirclement. Later in the afternoon 3. *Fallschirmjaegerdivision* made another assault from inside the pocket. Co-ordinated with other German attacks, temporary escape routes from the pocket were opened north and south of the ridge along the D242 and D16 enabling some 5,000 survivors of 3. *Fallschirmjaegerdivision* led by General Eugen Meindl, commander of 2 *Fallschirmjaegerkorps* to make their escape. Perhaps this is the grave of one of his *fallschirmjaegers* who fell during this action. (PISM)

V

The Pursuit

For 21st Army Group the immediate period after Normandy was known as the "Great Swan". Borrowing this phrase from those who had experienced the long advances (and retreats) during the North African campaign, some British armoured units advancing from Normandy recorded daily advances of 26 miles a day. This was impressive, compared to the limited advances that had been achievable during the intense combat in Normandy. For the Germans the period following their defeat in France was known as "the Void" when all that could be done once they had evacuated their surviving forces over the Seine, was to fall back to the borders of the *Reich*. Small rearguards attempted to try and slow down the pursuing Allies, and ports along the Channel Coast were declared Fortresses and their garrisons ordered to hold out for as long as possible to prevent their use by the Allies.

The 1st Polish Armoured Division did not immediately join in this advance. Its immediate priority to was to replace both personnel and equipment losses. The division had suffered 1,441 casualties in Normandy and making these up was difficult. As had been planned before Normandy, Poles who had been conscripted into the German Army and had been captured by their fellow Poles were invited to join the division. Although this policy did replace casualties, concerns were noted regarding the lack of training and medical problems. By December 1944 the division was short of 2,298 personnel.

After a short period in reserve the 1st Polish Armoured Division joined in the pursuit of the retreating German forces across northern France, as part of the II Canadian Corps, operating on the right flank of the Canadian Army. Moving to Elbeuf where the divisional engineers constructed a Bailey Bridge across the Seine which was named "The Warsaw Bridge". First across on 29 August was the divisional armoured reconnaissance regiment the 10th Motor Rifles which operated in the van of the division. The destruction of their forces in the Falaise Pocket meant that that there was no hope of the Germans being able to establish a line of defence along the Seine and their forces fell back towards the next major river, the Somme. The German *15. Armee* had occupied the line of the river in the Canadian sector and had destroyed the bridges, before being forced to fall back in the face of the rapid advance of the Second British Army on its left.

To press the advance, 4th Canadian Armoured Division was ordered to establish a bridgehead at Pont Remy and the 1st Polish Armoured Division another at Abbeville, approximately five miles downstream.

The Poles advanced rapidly and approached Abbeville on 2 September. As the Polish tanks moved into the suburbs towards the ruins of a wrecked railway bridge the Germans blew the other bridge over the river. Although some infantry were able to make an improvised crossing, the tanks were unable to follow, until a temporary bridge had been constructed, but provided fire support from the other side of the river. Heavy exchanges of fire across the river from camouflaged German artillery positions forced the Polish tanks to regularly shift their location. The infantry who had managed to cross came under fire from snipers who had taken up positions in the town and in the towers of the Church of Saint Wulfran. During the night of the 2– 3 September, infantrymen from the 8th and 9th battalions managed to cross the Somme Canal using small boats. Eventually some three infantry battalions were able to fight their way into the town, capturing a large body of prisoners in the process. At about 10.00 in the morning, tanks were able to move forward in their support over a temporary bridge constructed by the divisional engineers.

Upstream the 4th Canadian Armoured Division had secured their bridgehead at Pont Remy and their tanks began to cross on 3 September.

The Poles now took the lead of the II Canadian Corps advance and drove northward from their bridgehead meeting scattered resistance. On the 5 September the 1st Polish Armoured Division liberated St Omer. On 6 September the division crossed the Franco-Belgian frontier and overcame enemy resistance at Ypres. Thanks to their liberation by the Poles, with heavy fighting still continuing around the town, the inhabitants of Ypres immediately resumed the tradition, prohibited by the German occupation authorities, of playing the Last Post in honour of the forces of the British Empire who fought there during the First World War (a ceremony which has since continued uninterrupted to this day). Following the liberation of Thielt (8 September) the 'Pursuit' ground to a halt. The Division had covered approximately 290 miles during the last 11 days. However German resistance had began to stiffen and the countryside favoured the defense. Both weather and terrain hampered the Polish advance with a battlefield riven by canals and dykes. The Division began to prepare for the coming autumn and winter campaign and the battles they would fight in the coming months in the Netherlands and Germany and the realisation that even then, they were 'Daleko do Domu' (far from home).

The Pursuit

219. *Panzerwerfer 42*, **Tostes, France, 23 August 1944**. A Cromwell passes a damaged and abandoned German 15cm *Panzerwerfer 42 auf Selbstfahrlafette* Sd.Kfz. 4/1, while another soldier examines it more closely. The *Panzerwerfer 42* was a multiple launch rocket system, inspired by the successful use of the Red Army's *Katyusha* mobile rocket launchers. Although less accurate than artillery it could cover a wider area and often have a demoralizing effect on its targets. This vehicle is probably from 7.*Werfer Brigade,* one of three deployed in Normandy, mainly against the British and Canadians. On average a brigade had between 90 – 132 launch vehicles. (PISM)

220. 10th Dragoons, France, August 1944. Dispatch riders from the 10th Dragoons make contact with civilians. Note the motor bike on the right, has a 54 tactical marking (10th Dragoons) and PL (Poland) on it's rear wheel arch and a Allied recognition star painted on the casing adjcent. The 10th Dragoons was the Motor Battalion attached to the 10th Armoured Cavalry Brigade. Dispatch riders served a vital function in passing messages between various units and headquarters, their motor bikes providing a capability to move quickly over cross-country. The two riders are wearing protective helmets and are carrying 9mm Sten Mk III 9mm sub-machine guns for personal protection. They are riding M20 motor-bikes, the standard British motor-cycle of World War II with 126,000 made. They were made by BSA (Birmingham Small Arms) at one stage in its history the world's largest manufacturer of motorcycles. (PISM)

221. Bailey Bridge, Elbeuf, France, August 1944. Polish Engineers work on assembling a Bailey Bridge over the Seine at Elbeuf. The bridge was designed to be easily portable in pre-fabricated steel and wooden parts, which could be manhandled into position without the need of specialist tools or equipment. The engineers in the foreground are dragging a 10 foot long crossed-braced side panel from a truck. Each of these panels weighed 570 pounds and could be lifted by six men. In the background a number of the panels have already been fixed together to form the sides of the bridge. The other objects in the photo are the components that will be used to form a roadway across the completed bridge. Although some of the engineers wear steel helmets, the majority are not, indicating that there is no immediate threat to the operation from artillery or air attack. (PISM)

222. Bailey Bridge and Cromwell, Elbeuf, France, 29 August 1944. The completed Bailey Bridge in operation. A Cromwell tank from the 10th Mounted Rifles crosses the bridge to the north bank. The sign on the right carries the divisional insignia in the centre, flanked by the Arm of Service number for the 10th (46) and 11th (41) Field Company Engineers who carried out the construction, together with the 1st Bridging Platoon. The sign also carries the directional message "To Warsaw". This must have had a particular poignancy to the bridge's builders, and those crossing the bridge, because at this time the Germans were suppressing, with great ruthlessness, the Warsaw Uprising (1 August – 2 October 1944) launched by the Polish Home Army. As the divisional reconnaissance regiment the 10th Mounted Rifles would lead the advance of the division as it headed towards its next objective, Abbeville. (PISM)

223. *Jagdpanther*, **Elbeuf, France, 25 August 1944.** A *Jagdpanther* from *schwere Panzerjager-Abteilung 654*, the only unit of *Jagdpanthers* to fight in Normandy. Although some of the unit's *Jagdpanthers* were ferried across the Seine to safety, three vehicles from its 1.*Kompanie* were stuck in traffic jams on the southern bank of the river unable to cross and therefore, like this vehicle commanded by *Feldwebel* Siebels, were blown up. (PISM).

224. Sherman ARV I, Sommery, France, September, 1944. A column of tanks and armoured vehicles move through the French countryside towards Abbeville. Leading the column are a number of Sherman tanks. The tracked vehicle second from the right is a Sherman Armoured Recovery Vehicle (ARV) I. A converted standard tank (minus the turret) this provided a means of recovering disabled tanks from the battlefield. In Normandy each Polish armoured squadron had a Sherman ARV I attached to its 4th platoon. Moving up behind the ARV is a M5 half-track, probably part of the armoured regiment's Light Aid Detachment which provided basic repair and maintenance for the unit's armoured vehicles. (PISM)

225. Wittes, Northern France, 5 September 1944. (Sequential photos 225-227.) During the advance to Saint Omer the 10th Dragoons were given the task of clearing the town of Wittes, but after suffering casualties had to be reinforced by a Cromwell platoon from 2nd Squadron, 10th Mounted Rifles. During this action Corporal Mastuszak and Private Korta were killed and Cadet Officer Klobukowski badly wounded. Here, in the aftermath of the action, local civilians mingle with the soldiers and the casualties lie, covered by groundsheets, alongside the Cromwell tank on the right of the picture (this might have been their vehicle). Another Cromwell can be seen on the left. In the background is a camouflaged German 8.8cm FLAK 18 or 36. This is probably part of the German defending force that engaged the Polish tanks. (PISM)

226. Wittes, Northern France, 5 September 1944. A viewpoint from behind the 75mm gun of the left hand Cromwell in the preceding image. The casualties are covered by groundsheets and two soldiers are examining the tank in the background which was probably damaged during the action. Note that track links have been added to its front hull to improve armour protection. The machine-gunner/co-driver of the foreground tank is in his position immediately to the front, on the left hand side of the tank. The barrel of his Besa 7.92 mm hull-mounted machine-gun can just be seen. The two standing figures behind the gun barrel may be other members of this tank's crew. The one on the left seems to be wearing a leather jerkin. Another tank crewman wearing the Royal Armoured Corps issue helmet moves across from the left. Most of the other figures in the photo would appear to be tank crew in coveralls and berets, but there are a number of soldiers wearing steel helmets who are almost certainly part of the 10th Dragoons the Cromwells were supporting. (PISM)

227. Wittes, France, 5 September 1944. A Polish officer conducts a burial service, attended by soldiers from both the 10th Mounted Rifles and the 10th Dragoons, for their fallen comrades. Local civilians have also come to pay their respects for those who died in their liberation. A French tricolour can be seen displayed on the building in the background. On the right of the picture are the two grave markers marking the temporary resting place for Corporal Mastuszak and Private Korta. The rear of a Cromwell can be seen at the left of the picture, and soldiers are standing on another to the rear. A further Cromwell is positioned behind the abandoned 8.8 cm FLAK gun. The bareheaded soldier in the foreground appears to be wearing a leather jerkin. The 10th Dragoons soldier on the ground, below the soldier standing on the Cromwell is carrying a German stick grenade in his belt. (AHA)

228. Sherman V, Saint Omer France, 5 September 1944. A Sherman Mk. V makes its way over a Bailey Bridge constructed by the divisional engineers. The destroyed span of the original bridge can be seen in the background. In its advance across Northern France the 1st Polish Armoured Division had to bridge a number of water obstacles, large and small. The division's engineers had already bridged the Dives at Jort, the Seine at Elbeuf, the Somme at Abbeville and now the As at Saint Omer. The Germans did not offer much resistance, but as they fell back they systematically demolished every bridge to delay the advancing Polish and Canadian forces. A staff officer commented that "the problem facing II Canadian Corps at the moment is not German soldiers but bridging difficulties". (PISM)

229. **FLAK Gun**, **France, Normandy, August, 1944**. German *Flugzeugabwerkanone* (Flak) antiaircraft gun, either a 8.8 cm Flak 18 or 36. Also effectively used in the anti-tank role, this one appears to have been blown up by its crew, judging by the barrel and breech damage. (AHA).

230. **German Ammunition**, **France, Normandy, August, 1944**. Discarded and broken German ammunition boxes and shells lie in the undergrowth. The inscription on the box indicates that this is an ammunition case for 8.8 cm rounds carried by the Tiger I tank. The lettering on the lid of the wooden box is as follows. *Patr.* is the German military abbreviation for *Patrone*, which means "round" or "shell". *Kw.k* is the abbreviation for *KampfwagenKanone* (tank gun). *KampfwagenKanone Kw.K.36* is the designation for the gun mounted on the Tiger I tank (*Panzerkampfwagen VI Tiger Ausf. E*). An intact round, probably an armour-piercing *Panzergranate PzGr.39* lies below the box. Other ammunition rounds are also visible. (PISM)

231. **Former German Soldiers**, **France, August-September 1944**. A party of former German soldiers leave a PoW camp to join the Polish Army. After the 1939 invasion certain areas of Poland were incorporated into the *Reich* with their military-aged male citizens becoming liable for conscription. The result was large numbers of Poles serving in German military units. As Polish forces serving with the 8th Army advanced across North Africa and into Italy they began capturing fellow countrymen who had been fighting on the opposing side. The Poles were able to persuade very many of them to join them, thus filling gaps in their own ranks. The 1st Armoured Division decided to adopt a similar practice. Note these former prisoners have removed the *Wehrmacht* eagle from their jackets. PISM)

232. **Former German Soldiers**, **France, August-September 1944**. The group seen in the preceding photo has been transferred to the Polish military authorities, and seem happy and relaxed with their change of status. The Polish soldier on the extreme left, seems to be offering a cigarette to the smiling ex-prisoner to his left, while his immediate comrades seem to be looking on with amused interest. Perhaps hoping for one themselves! (PISM)

233. New Polish Army Recruits, France, August-September, 1944. Their old *Wehrmacht* uniforms discarded, now wearing newly-issued British battledress and Polish berets the new recruits to the 1st Polish Armoured Division march off to join their assigned units. During the Normandy Campaign the Division had suffered 1,441 casualties so these men are very welcome reinforcements. Despite such measures, manpower shortages would continue to be of serious concern to the division for the rest of the campaign. (PISM)

234. Jagdpanther, North-Western Europe, autumn 1944. A captured *Jagdpanther* sits undamaged in a vehicle collecting point for enemy vehicles. This is a late production model (May 1944) with a sectional barrel for its 8.8 cm Pak 43.3 L/71. Immediately behind, to the left is another *Jagdpanther* and in the background various other German tanks including a Panzer IV/70 (V). In the fighting to come in Belgium and Holland during the autumn of 1944 the Poles would rarely encounter *panzers*. Most armoured engagements being with *Sturmgeschutz* assault guns and self-propelled *Panzerjagers*, of which the *Jagdpanther* was the most formidable. (AHA)

235. Marder III, Northern France, August 1944. A German *Panzerjager* (tank hunter) 38(t) 7.5, Pak 40/3 aus H *Marder III*, based on the chassis of the obsolete Czech (CKD) *LT vz 38* tank and built from late 1942 to early 1943 to counter the ever increasing numbers of enemy tanks on the Eastern Front. This modified type had a different fighting compartment and the German Pak 40 instead of the captured Soviet 7.62 gun, from its predecessor. This one appears to have broken down, note tow ropes (see photo 236) as this is the same vehicle positioned behind the Panzer IV/70 (V). The open fighting compartment left much to be desired as the crew were exposed to overhead bursts and aircraft strafing as well as the weather. Further the thin armour only offered minimal protection against small arms and the PaK 40's huge muzzle blast exposed the vehicle's position so hit and run tactics had to be employed. Note Balkan cross on lower side panel, beneath vehicle number.(AHA)

236. *Panzer* IV/70 (V), Northern France, August 1944. A *Panzer* IV/70 (V) stands abandoned with a number of other vehicles on a wooded road in north-west Europe. Based on a Panzer IV chassis, with added protection provided by the use of sloped armour and a low silhouette this vehicle was an improved version of the *Jagdpanzer* IV. Introduced in August 1944 the Panzer IV/70 (V) mounted the same 75mm gun as the PzKw V Panther. Behind it can be seen the *Marder* featured in the previous image. (AHA)

237. Churchill AVRE, Normandy, France, August 1944. A Churchill AVRE (Armoured Vehicle Royal Engineers). As part of their preparations for the invasion of Europe, the British Army developed a range of specialist armoured vehicles (colloquially known as "Funnies") to assist in overcoming enemy defensive positions. Many were conversions of the Churchill tank. The AVRE variant mounted a 290mm spigot mortar which fired a 40lb demolition charge, designed for the rapid destruction of fortifications. All such specialist vehicles were under the control of the 79th Armoured Division which allocated them to assault divisions as required. One of the post-Normandy tasks of the 1st Canadian Army was the capture of those Channel ports still being held by the Germans. AVREs were essential in providing support to those troops attacking these heavily defended objectives. (PISM)

238. Pak 43, North-Western Europe, autumn 1944. A knocked-out German Pak 43 8.8cm anti-tank gun on a low silhouette mounting, one of its two axle limbers can be seen on the left. It had an effective range of 4,000 metres which enabled penetration of heavily armoured Allied vehicles at long ranges, especially those encountered on the Eastern Front. (AHA)

239. Sherman V and Firefly, Alphen, Holland, 5 October 1944. In the foreground is a Sherman Mk V with "applique" armour added to turret and hull sides. Note the Allied star has been toned-down to prevent it being used as a targeting point by enemy gunners (a lesson learned from the fighting in Normandy). The tank in the background is a Sherman Firefly with its barrel disguised to conceal its length as they were a priority target for German gunners (another lesson learned in Normandy). After a fierce battle the town was finally taken that evening by 2nd Armoured Regiment, supported by 9th Rifle Battalion, after a wedge had been driven into the enemy defences, splitting their forces. (AHA)

240. Pak 97/38, North-Western Europe, autumn 1944. A knocked-out German PaK 97/38 anti-tank gun with its dead crew. Partly obscured by the large tree, a soldier may be talking with an unseen member of the crew of the Humber Scout Car. A Stuart light tank moves past in the background. The Pak 97/38 was a German Army expedient to meet the increased demands for effective anti-tank guns on the Eastern Front. Barrels from captured French 75mm field guns were mounted on the carriage of the 5.cm Pak 38. To reduce the recoil a Swiss Solothurn muzzle brake was added. (PISM)

241. Sherman Vs and German Prisoners, Northern France, September 1944. A tank commander (centre between the PoWs) from 24th *Uhlans* questions captured Germans while the crew of the other tanks look on. He holds a pistol as a precaution and wears his beret in the Polish style, pulled back. The nearest Sherman V displays the "PL" nationality marking and the Arm of Service marking "53" indicating 24th *Uhlans*. This image is probably post-Normandy as both the Polish soldiers and their prisoners are wearing warmer clothing than they would have done some weeks before. One of the crew of the nearest tank is wearing a leather coat. (PISM).

242. General Maczek and Cromwell Command Tank, Northern France September 1944. General Maczek in the turret of his command tank (possibly in Abbelville). Like many other contemporary armour commanders (on both sides) he realised the importance of leading from the front and often directed operations from his personal command tank. The tank is a Cromwell Command tank. The main gun was removed and replaced by a dummy barrel. Extra radios were fitted, two No 19 sets and two No 38 sets which enabled the General to maintain contact both with his forward units and with his main headquarters to the rear. General Maczek's Cromwell carried the name "Hela" inscribed on the right hand side of the turret. Both the tank commander and General Maczek are wearing googles and berets, though the tank commander has ensured his Royal Armoured Corps helmet is close at hand. General Maczek's badges of rank are prominently displayed and the divisional insignia can be seen on his left sleeve. (PISM)

Appendix

Order Of Battle 1st Polish Armoured Division North-West Europe 1944-45

Divisional Headquarters and Divisional Support
10th Mounted Rifle Regiment (Reconnaissance)
Traffic Control Squadron, Field Court, Field Post Office, Quartermaster, Chaplain, Provost, Field Security, Paymaster, Reserve Tank Squadron, Reserve Infantry Company.

Armoured Brigade – 10th Armoured Cavalry Brigade
HQ
1st Armoured Regiment
2nd Armoured Regiment
24th Uhlan (Lancers) Regiment
10th Dragoons Regiment

Infantry Brigade – 3rd Rifle Brigade
HQ
1st Podhale (Highland) Rifle Battalion
8th Rifle Battalion
9th Rifle Battalion
1st Independent Heavy Machine-Gun Squadron

Divisional Artillery
HQ
1st Motorised Artillery Regiment (Self-Propelled)
2nd Motorised Artillery Regiment (Towed)
1st Anti -Tank Artillery Regiment
1st Anti – Aircraft Artillery Regiment

Divisional Engineers
HQ
10th Field Company Engineers
11th Field Company Engineers
Field Park Company
Bridge Platoon

Divisional Signals-1st Signals Battalion
HQ Squadron
1st, 2nd, 3rd, 10th Signals Squadrons

Divisional Workshops
3rd & 10th Workshop Companies

Divisional Medical Units
10th Light Field Ambulance
11th Heavy Field Ambulance
1st Field Dressing Station
1st Field Hygiene Station

Divisonal Supply Units
3rd Transport Company (Ammunition)
10th Transport Company (Petrol)
11th Transport Company (Rations)
Infantry Transport Company

Bibliography & Correspondence

CORRESPONDENCE
Tony Begg
Henry Budzynski
Peter Cosgrove
Peter Dennis
Greg Hall
Chris Lock
Evan McGilvray
Andrej Mazur
Paul Middeton
David Paintin
Peter Sikora
Joseph Smith
Łukasz Stożek
Richard Szczawinski
Ken Tout

BIBLIOGRAPHY
1st Polish Armoured Division (1 VIII 1944 – 11 XI 1944) France-Belgium-Holland. Breda-Osterhout, Louis Vermijs N.V., n.d.
1st Polish Armoured Division, Muzeum Wojska Polskiego, Bellona, 2014.
1 Pułku Pancerny w Latach 1939-1946, Hanover, 1946. *Śladami Polskich Gąsienic 1939-1947,* Edipresse-Kolekcje sp.z.o.o. Warszawa 2014.
Archer, Lee & Auerbach, William, *Panzerwrecks 11, Normandy 2,* New York, Panzerwrecks, 2010.
Barbarksi, Krzysztof, *Polish Armour 1939-45 (Osprey Vanguard 30),* London, Osprey Publishing, 1982.
Buckley, John, *British Armour in Normandy,* London, Frank Cass, 2004.
Darby, Hugh and Cunliffe, Marcus, *A Short History of 21st Army Group,* Aldershot, Gale and Polden Ltd, 1949.
Florentin, Eddy, *The Battle of the Falaise Gap,* London, Elek Books, 1965.
Ford, Ken, *Falaise 1944, death of an army (Osprey Campaign 149),* Oxford, Osprey, 2009.
Jamar, K, *With the Tanks of the 1st Polish Armoured Division,* Hengelo, H.L. Smit & Zn, 1946.
Jackowski, Grzegorz, *Wozy bojowe Wojska Polskiego 1939,* Warszawa, Wydawnictwo "Militaria", 2012.
Jarymowycz, Roman, *Tank Tactics; from Normandy to Lorraine,* Mechanicsburg, Stackpole Books, 2001.
Jarzembowski, Janusz, *Armoured Hussars; Images of the Polish 1st Armoured Division 1939-47,* Solihull, Helion & Company, 2014.
Kaminski, Andrzej Antoni, *Od "Acromy" do "Zwyciezcy",* Malopolska Poligrafia, Krakow, n.d.
Koszutski, Stanisław, *Wspomnienia z różnych pobojowisk,* London, n.p., 1972.
Lalak, Zbigniew, *Polish Armoured Forces 1939-1945, Organisation and Order of Battle,* Warsaw, Pegas-Bis & O.K. Media, 2005.
Latawski, Paul, *Falaise Pocket (Battle Zone Normandy),* Stroud, Sutton Publishing, 2004.
Lodieu, Didier, *La Massue: Les Soldats Polonais dans la Bataille de Normandie,* Ysec Editions, 2007.
McGilvray, Evan, *The Black Devils' March, A Doomed Odyssey – the 1st Polish Armoured Division 1939-45,* Solihull, Helion & Company, 2005.
McGilvray, Evan, *Man of Steel and Honour – General Stanislaw Maczek, Soldier of Poland, Commander of the 1st Polish Armoured Division in North-West Europe 1944-45,* Solihull, Helion & Company, 2012.
Majka, Jerzy, *Invincible Black Brigade, Polish 10th Cavalry Brigade 1939,* Sandomierz, Mushroom Model Publications, 2010.
Meyer, Hubert, *The 12th SS: the history of the Hitler Youth Panzer Division, Volume Two,* Mechanicsburg, Stackpole Books, 2005.

Mieczkowski, Zbigniew, *The Soldiers of General Maczek in World War II*, Foundation for the Commemoration of General Maczek First Polish Armoured Division.Warsaw, MATRIX, 2004.

Pallud, Jean Paul, *Ruckmarsch! the German retreat from Normandy then and now*, Harlow, Battle of Britain Publishers, 2006.

Prados, John, *Normandy Crucible: the decisive battle that shaped Work War II in Europe*, New York, NAL Caliber, 2012.

Reid, Brian A., *No Holding Back: Operation Totalize, Normandy, August 1944*, Mechanicsburg, Stackpole Books, 2009.

Tout, Ken, *Tank! 40 Hours of Battle, August 1944,* Stroud, Sutton, 1998.

Wiatrowski, Tadeusz, *2nd Polish Armoured Regiment in Action, From Caen to Wilhelmshaven.* Hanover, Schlutersche Buchdruckerei, 1946.

The Polish Institute and Sikorski Museum
20 Prince's Gate, London SW7 1PT

www.pism.co.uk
Tel.: 0207 589 9249

Since 1945 the single largest museum and archive devoted to the Polish Government in Exile and the Polish Armed Forces in Europe outside of Poland.

The Museum covers three floors of exhibits chronicling Poland's military and cultural history from the XVII century to 1945 with emphasis on the 20th century. It also has a large Photographic, Film and Audio Archive.

The Archives which span the period 1860-1990 cover 1.5 klm of shelving and contain a unique documentation of Poland's political and military history during the 20th century concentrating on the Second World War, including fascinating insights into Anglo-Polish military relations at the time and of the major political and military British and Allied personalities.

These collections are currently being digitalised and being made available online.

There are over 100,000 pages of documents and a growing number of films as well as many of the archival finding aids online. To see them visit our website on: www.pism.co.uk

Opening times:
MUSEUM: Tuesday-Friday: 2pm – 4pm
1st Saturday of the month: 10.30am – 4pm

ARCHIVE READING ROOM: Tuesday to Friday: 9.30am – 4pm
(Closed throughout February)

Prior booking of a place in the reading room is required: 00 44 207 589 9249